Endorsements

A Teen's Guide to Finding a Job is easy to follow with step-by-step directions to employment success. Naomi Vernon has taken the mystery out of the job-hunting process. It's hard enough for teens to face the reality that finding a job is a crucial part of becoming a self-sufficient adult. This book makes the task more manageable. Teens can move ahead with confidence through the insight provided in *A Teen's Guide to Finding a Job.*

> — *Dr. Sheila D. White-Daniels,*
> *College Administrator*
> *Higher Education Consultant*

As a parent, *A Teen's Guide to Finding a Job* was a godsend. When my teenagers told me they wanted to find jobs, instead of giving them advice from when I got my first job, I let an expert give them the most up-to-date information. It was invaluable!

> — *D. Wiss,*
> *Parent of job-seeking teen*

After I graduated from high school, I had no clue what direction to take. Luckily, this book gave me the knowledge *and* the tools to guide me down the path to finding a stable job. Following the advice in the 60-second introduction gave me the confidence to talk to employers. Because of it, I landed an interview for the top job on my list.

> — *Taylor Pefferkorn,*
> *New Job Seeker*

As a teenager looking for a well-paying summer job, I found *A Teen's Guide to Finding a Job* informative, direct, easy to comprehend, and useful. Not only does it clearly outline the process on how to obtain a job, it also holds useful tips on how to maintain the job, and even how to resign if need be.

In reading this book, I found what I had expected (i.e., an outline of the application process, how to find jobs in your area, how to determine your interests, etc.). I also found what I did not expect, such as how body language can affect your chances in an interview, or how using negative words or dressing sloppily can turn off a potential employer. I feel that reading *A Teen's Guide to Finding a Job* prepared me extremely well for the job application process. The skills and tips found in it cannot only be used now but also later on in life.

— *Lily Wiss,*
High School Student

Once I started reading *A Teen's Guide to Finding a Job,* my mind opened and my confidence increased. Following examples, I prepared my résumé and began my job search. On this go 'round, employers responded differently toward me, asking me to fill out applications and stay to interview. Thank goodness, I'd read Chapter 5! Plus, I had used the author's tips about how to be dressed and presentable. I was given the job and also complimented on how I was dressed. The tips also helped me control my nervousness.

In addition, this book greatly helped me with money management. When I had my first job, I'd openly spend money on shopping sprees as if I had an unlimited supply. I now know to focus on the necessities.

I would definitely recommend this book to teens starting their working careers.

— *Fred Morris III,*
High School Student

After reading this life-changing book, I was able to network and approach employers with confidence. The part on applying for federal employment increased my awareness of summer job options and federal employment as a career.

— Penny Perry,
High School Student

I'm a single parent always looking for resources to prepare my child for life's challenges. *A Teen's Guide to Finding a Job* was the answer to my prayers. I served in the United States Air Force as a personnelist. For many years, I experienced first-hand the emotional stress adults encounter dealing with the job-search process. I wanted to introduce my child early to tools that would prepare him for one of life's unavoidable challenges—looking for employment.

This guide explains the job-search process from start to finish. It even provides information on creating your own job by introducing young people to entrepreneurship. Plus it discusses the impact social media (Facebook, Twitter, MySpace, LinkedIn, and blogging) can have on a job search—something all teens need to be aware of. This guide put my son on the right track—both with his job and in our relationship.

— Fred Morris, Jr.,
MSgt Fred Morris, Jr, USAF, Retired and parent

A Teen's Guide to Finding a JOB

Naomi Vernon
Job Search Coach

Third Edition

New Beeginnings, San Antonio, Texas

ISBN: 978-0-9676383-1-7 (e-book)
ISBN: 978-0-9676383-0-0 (Paperback)

This book is printed on acid-free paper.

Because of the dynamic nature of the Internet, any web
addresses or links contained in this book may have
changed since publication and may no longer be valid.

NU-B Publishing

Whom You'll Meet Inside:

Chris   Nikki   David   Candiss   Sophia   Carlos

We are just like you, traveling this journey and searching for the ideal career path as we read *A Teen's Guide to Finding a Job* to find our way.

What You'll Learn Inside:

Self-assessment	Résumé Writing
Employment Application	Employer's Perspective
Interviewing Techniques	What to Do With Your Money
Salary Negotiation	How to Quit a Job
Research Tips	Entrepreneurship

This book is dedicated to:

America's youth, who are faced with the challenge of finding the means to earn money or secure gainful employment.

You'll find the information, techniques, and exercises in this book—when put to practice—will develop skills to serve you well throughout your work life.

May you learn how to "fish" so others won't need to "give you a fish" again.

Introduction

A *Teen's Guide to Finding a Job* is written for America's youth who are uncertain about their career goals or objectives—teens needing assistance with choosing a rewarding career path that fits their interests, skills, and abilities.

This all-inclusive guide introduces them to the career exploration process ranging from self-awareness to suitable employment options. Used properly, it will put them on the path to finding the right career for them.

Specifically, this comprehensive guide provides the tools needed for teens to find their first job on the path of their ultimate career choice. It also introduces them to various careers, enabling them to "try before buying." Early exposure increases their chances of choosing the right career the first time.

Indeed, the guidance here applies to both those planning to go to college and those who want to start their work careers now. Use it to help understand the *job search process* and all its elements.

About the Author

Naomi Vernon was a teen mom who has beat all odds. After earning a master's degree in human resources development from Webster University, she has worked in the human resources field ever since.

For many years, Naomi assisted U.S. military personnel in making the transition from the military to civilian workforce. Today, she works for the federal government in Washington D.C. as a career management officer.

Naomi has dedicated her life to preparing youth for the challenge of finding employment. She has volunteered hundreds of hours helping teens build their job search skills.

Specifically, she introduces them to the *job search process* so they can build confidence while learning the skills needed to secure employment. She helps increase their awareness of the working world and inspires them to go after their dreams. Naomi's three adult children—now successful professionals in the criminal justice field—are living proof of her guidance and influence.

The author of *A Teen's Guide to Finding a Job* firmly believes that an early introduction to life skills will help teens develop a lifelong practical mindset. To that end, this guide includes valuable tools and practices for transforming their dreams into reality.

As she says, "Preparation is the stepping stone to success!"

Your 30-Second Networking Commercial 30
Networking Tips 30
Career Fairs 33
Career Fair Preparation 34
Career Fair Do's 34
Career Fair Don'ts 35
Your 60-Second Introduction 36

Chapter 3: The Employment Application Process **39**
Employment Application 41
Personal Appearance 43
Content of the Application 44
Validity of the Application 44
Completing an Employment Application 45
Sample Application Form 51
Verbs and Power Words 54
Tips and Reminders 66
Follow-up Action 67
Work Permit 68
You Can Do It! 69
Jobs You Can Apply For 70

Chapter 4: Résumés **75**
Résumé Formats 77
What Job Do You Want? 79
Getting Started 80
Writing Your Résumé 81
Choosing a Format 88
The Chronological Résumé 88
The Functional Résumé 91
The Combination Résumé 94
Résumé Guidelines 97
Writing a Federal Résumé 99

Writing a Cover Letter 104
Preparing a Reference Sheet 108

Chapter 5: Interviewing **113**
The Interviewing Process 115
Interviewing Strategies 118
Research 118
Written Materials 119
Networking 119
Social Media 120
"Acing" the Interview 122
Interview Questions 123
Frequently Asked Questions 124
Forbidden Interview Questions 126
Behavior Interview Questions 130
General Tips and Guidelines 132
Preparing Thank-you Letters 133
Body of Your Thank-you Letter 133

Chapter 6: The Employer's Perspective **137**
Application and Résumé Do List: 139
The Interview Do List: 140
The Application Don't List 141
The Interview Don't List 142
After-You-Are-Hired Don't List 143
Words of Wisdom and Encouraging Messages 144
Job Search Skills 146
Advice to Keep in Mind 149

Chapter 7: Salary Negotiation **151**
Work Values 154
Personal Values 154
How to Negotiate 156

Good Ethical Practices 156
Know What You Value 157
Value Exercise: Work and Personal Values Important
    to You 158
Values Employers Look for in Employees 160

**Chapter 8: Now I'm Making Money, What Do I
Do With It?** **163**
Good Money-management Rules 166
Managing Your Money. 168
Money Smart Vocabulary. 175

Chapter 9: If You Must Quit a Job. **177**

Chapter 10: Entrepreneurship and You **183**
Qualities and Traits of Successful Entrepreneurs 185
Starting Your Own Business 186
Actions to Take Before Starting a Business 187
Helpful Resources. 190
Entrepreneurship Education 193
Stories from Young Entrepreneurs .193
Famous Entrepreneurs Who Started in their Teens 201
In Closing 206

Conclusion **207**

Acknowledgements **211**

CHAPTER 1

Self-assessment Tools

Sophia

Sophia

Sophia is a 17-year-old senior in high school who has two younger siblings she takes care of after school. Her mother, a single parent, juggles two jobs to support the family. Sophia picks up her siblings from school, prepares dinner, and helps them with their homework, and she still finds time to get her own homework done.

Sophia's ultimate career goal is to become a pharmacist. She knows the importance of making good grades in math, science, and biology but is unsure of how to map out a career path to become a pharmacist.

Currently, Sophia is struggling in chemistry and knows she needs a tutor. She discussed her concerns with her chemistry teacher. They both agreed she needed a tutor, taking into account her after-school responsibilities. But because Sophia asked for help and was not afraid to admit she needed it, her teacher agreed to tutor her during the lunch hour.

Sophia wants to be a good example for her siblings and not struggle like her mother does as an adult. She's always thinking of ways to make things better.

She also visited the school guidance counselor to talk about her dream to become a pharmacist. The guidance counselor suggested she take a self-assessment to get a better understanding of her likes and dislikes, and to learn how she might react to certain situations. The counselor understood the value in Sophia knowing those things; she knew it would help her map out a career path to achieve her ultimate career goal.

Also, Sophia and the counselor discussed the need for Sophia to make money while working on advancing her education after graduation. They both agreed that the results of the self-assessment will also provide employment options for Sophia to explore—options that will get her steps closer to becoming a pharmacist. As well, she can identify other employment opportunities in the health care career field while pursuing her education.

Sophia quickly learned the value of a self-assessment and how it could help her map out a career plan.

Overview

What's the first thing to do? You can begin by taking a self-assessment to inventory your skills, talents, interests, knowledge, abilities, work values, and personal traits. It will increase your awareness of the skills you're already using at home, in school, and in the community. Ultimately, it helps you match yourself to a job or career most suitable for your personality.

Knowing who you are and how you fit into the work world will help you select a rewarding job and career. Plus a self-assessment will prevent you from making choices based on *someone else's values or expectations.*

Some self-assessment tools may simply require answering a series of questions, requiring no right or wrong answers. Your scores are based on a *pattern* of answers that emerges, not your answer to any particular question.

Your choice of answers should reflect what you actually do and feel, so be honest; there is no way you can fail.

Most important, self-assessment results will provide you with options to explore. They'll reveal information about you that you're probably not aware of or that you haven't valued before.

When applied properly, the information you glean from your assessment can play a major role in helping to find the job or career path that's right for you.

What's most important of all? Realizing what you feel passionate about and what services you have to offer.

What Self-assessments Can Do

A self-assessment helps by highlighting and connecting abilities you may not have seen as a source of employment or entrepreneurship. For example, some of your hobbies and talents may very well define the area you are best suited to pursue as a job or career.

A self-assessment also encourages self-exploration. Finding a job or career that is right for your personality will make you happy, fulfilled, and satisfied with your career choices.

Why are most people unhappy with their jobs? Often, they've taken a wrong turn due to lack of preparation and self-knowledge. They find themselves in jobs or careers that don't fit their personality, which may cause them to feel unhappy or even depressed.

That's why it's important to use a self-assessment. You want to identify your likes and dislikes, and your strengths and weaknesses. It will also give you a fairly accurate picture of how you relate to and interact with others. This information is invaluable in pointing you to jobs in various work environments. In addition, it compares your likes and dislikes to those of people who are successfully working in occupations you may consider.

What happens when you have similar interests to people successfully employed in a career field? Research has shown you'll gain satisfaction from working in that field as well.

What Self-assessments Can't Do

A self-assessment can't tell you what you are going to be. It can only provide you with information about careers best suited to you.

After all, you know yourself better than anyone else. To ensure you have a broader perspective, consult with trusted adults (your parents, a coach, a teacher, or a mentor) to gain objective feedback. They will most likely see potential in you that you've overlooked.

Compare the assessment results to what you know about yourself and what others have constructively shared with you. For example, you may have strong math skills, and your self-assessment results suggest you become a mathematician. However, you know you like working with people more than strictly numbers. That's a clue for you to explore your career options. You'll look for those jobs or careers that allow you to work with people while still using your math skills.

View your self-assessment results as an eye opener to give you choices you can explore, not hard-and-fast answers about who you will become. Only after completing your research should you begin making career decisions.

Types of Self-assessment Tools

Any of the assessments listed here provide powerful tools to help you become more aware of your skills, interests, work values, and personal traits.

Career Ability Placement Survey (CAPS)

The CAPS series of tests measures eight specific areas of ability: Mechanical Reasoning, Spatial Relations, Verbal Reasoning, Numerical Ability, Language Usage, Word Knowledge, Perceptual Speed and Accuracy, and Manual Speed and Dexterity.

Career Occupational Preference Survey (COPS) System

The COPS System measures abilities, interests, and values. The scores are related to 14 occupational groupings or clusters. It consists of a series of activities related to occupations. Answer the questions honestly based on your likes and dislikes.

This system is better used for college-bound and vocation-oriented people rather than people who are just looking for a job.

Career Orientation Placement And Evaluation Survey (COPES)

This survey is designed to measure personal values. Constructing a set of work values and qualities will help you choose a career with purpose and meaning for you. Think of work values as part of a larger framework of life values.

Educational Interest Inventory

This tool is designed to assist junior and senior high school students, freshman and sophomore college students, vocational and technical students, and adult continuing-education students. It assesses their interests and relates those interests to collegiate and vocational study.

Keirsey Temperament Sorter

This assessment is designed to identify different kinds of personality temperaments. It will help you understand yourself and others. The focus is on behavior that's directly observable whereas the Myers-Briggs Type Indicator primarily focuses on how people think and feel.

Myers-Briggs Type Indicator (MBTI)

MBTI assesses your personality type as well as identifies your preferences in perception and judgment. It can assist you in recognizing how you view situations and make decisions. It also helps you to understand your strengths, the type of work you might enjoy, and how others with different preferences can relate to and be of value to each other.

Knowing your personality-type profile will help you identify occupations that complement your nature and how you like to interact with others.

Self-Directed Search

This self-guided assessment helps you find the occupations and fields of study best suited to your interests and skills. You answer questions about preferred activities, competencies, occupations, and abilities. Based on your answers, you'll receive a three-letter summary code. The code tells you what occupations best suit your personality is and the types of work or training that match your interests.

The Strong Interest Inventory

This inventory gives you information about your interests in relation to the interests of people working actual occupations. The focus is to help you better understand yourself so you can make better decisions about selecting academic majors and careers.

Interest Determination, Exploration, And Assessment System (IDEAS)

IDEAS is designed for educational situations in which a short, relatively inexpensive, paper-and-pencil, self-scoring career exploration tool is required. It helps students with employment concerns when a quick, immediate overview of their interests is desired or required. Use IDEAS when your goal is to narrow the entire career field to two or three areas you're inclined to explore further.

Where to Get Self-assessment and Career Planning Information

Make your first stop your school guidance counselor. He or she will explain which assessments are available as well as the purpose of each. Your counselor can also suggest which assessment best identifies your needs and is most appropriate for your situation. Ask the counselor about other books and computer programs you can use to further explore your career interests. Your counselor can even help you select the classes needed to either prepare for your chosen field or continue your education—or both!

Where to Find Self-assessments

- High School Guidance Counselors
- Employment Agencies
- Career Centers
- Career Counselors
- Social Services Agencies
- Placement and Job Referral Services
- National Career Development Association (NCDA)
- Career Information Centers
- State Employment Services
- Public Libraries
- Online Self-assessments
- Assessment Books
- Counseling Services
- Community Centers
- Community Agencies
- One-Stop Career Centers

i'm going to...
ask questions
get advice
become more
focused

Online Self-assessment Resources

Careers By Design
Online Assessment Center that identifies general interests.
www.careers-by-design.com

Cook Consultants Designer and Facilitator
A career workshop for teens: MY COMPANY, INC.
Kcooknet@aol.com

JobHuntersBible.com
Excellent tool for researching companies and obtaining salary information with excellent site links.
www.jobhuntersbible.com/counseling

SIGI Plus for High School Students
Best for students looking for a job after graduation or planning to continue their education. The SIGI Plus will help put your career plans in order.
www.valparint.com/sigi3.htm

The Temperament Sorter II
Discover your personality temperament using this tool.
www.advisorteam.com/user/ktsintro.asp

Myers-Briggs Type Indicator (MBTI)
Personality Pathways
Learn about MBTI personality type concepts and various applications. Take a free online self-scoring personality test. The MBTI helps you understand preferences—both yours and others.
www.personalitypathways.com/type_inventory.html

Self-Directed Search

This is the most widely used career interest inventory. Discover Holland Code (RIASEC) and match your skills and interests to a job, career, training program, college major, or field of study. Each code (RIASEC) represents a type: Realistic (R) – Doers, Investigative (I) – Thinkers, Artistic (A) – Creators, Social (S) – Helpers, Enterprising (E) – Persuaders, Conventional (C) – Organizers.
www.surfnetkids.com/career.htm

Strong Interest Inventory

You can call and schedule an appointment to talk with a counselor. Your call will be returned, usually within 24 hours. A consultant will assess your needs, answer any questions you have about fees or services, and refer you to an expert.
www.virginiafamilycounseling.com/howtogetstarted.html

Tech Prep

This tool helps students to prepare for a "high-skill" career while still in high school. It provides a roadmap to identify and acquire academic and work-related skills.
www.careerplanner.com/Career-Test-Career-Search/Career-Test-for-Highschool-Students.cfm

There are many other self-assessment tools on the market, so take your time in selecting one or more that fits for you. Discuss the tools with your parents and/or mentor as well as your school guidance counselor. (Again, visiting your school's guidance counselor is a good first step.)

Your Personal Action Plan

I have completed my research and would like to complete a self-assessment:

_____
(Type of assessment)

I will contact _____
to schedule my appointment to take the assessment.

Date and time my self-assessment is scheduled for:

_____

My self-assessment results revealed:

_____

I am interested in the following: _____

_____

_____

I will research _____

_____

_____

This is the direction I plan to take: _____

_____

_____

_____

_____

My career choices are: _____

_____

_____

_____

_____

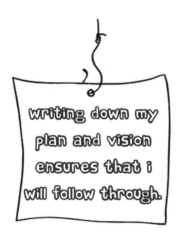

writing down my plan and vision ensures that i will follow through.

Self-assessments are important because you need to know who you are before you can decide what to become.

CHAPTER 2
Research

David

David

David is a high school senior interested in criminal justice careers. He's undecided about which job in the criminal justice field is best for him. But David knows he must research the field to narrow his options and do some career exploration. He's interested in learning career research techniques that will produce proven fruitful results.

David's goal is to gather career information on jobs in the criminal justice career field as well as various industries and companies. From there, he'll identify the education and training requirements he'll need.

He plans to use the information to make informed career choices and establish an effective job search plan. Specifically, he wants his first job to be on the criminal justice career path. He believes it will help build a solid foundation and increase future advancement opportunities when he goes into the workforce full time.

Therefore, he knows he must work a regular part-time job as a college student, and definitely on summer and holiday breaks. In this way, David is thinking ahead and plans to schedule an appointment with his freshmen orientation career counselor at college. He will seek the counselor's assistance to find work.

Also, after networking with friends, family, teachers, and a host of others, he decided to turn it up a notch and glean information from individuals working in the criminal justice field. He quickly discovered he'd get more accurate and valuable information by conducting informational interviews. He'll also attend career fairs targeting individuals in that field.

Through networking, doing informational interviews, and attending career fairs, David identified the best college to attend, learned about the challenges in his chosen career field, and established a networking system that will serve him well when he's ready to enter the workforce.

Clearly, David now has a better understanding than ever of how he can fit into the criminal justice career field!

Overview

After taking a self-assessment, you better understand how your interests, skills, abilities, and personal traits fit into the world of work. Research becomes your next step. Although the assessment you took identified areas of interest and provided career options, you're probably still not prepared to make a career choice. At this point, you likely have many more unanswered questions. What's the difference? The nature of your questions and their focus.

Chances are, before you did your self-assessment, you had not made the connection between your working self and the world of work. Now, you likely know the type of work you're interested in. Yet, before you make any career choices, it's best to weigh all the facts. You'll want to have a *complete* profile of the occupations you've selected before choosing.

Your goal is to learn as much as you can about the career field or job that interests you. That requires gathering information that will help you see the complete picture. Specifically, you want to research *higher education requirements, related occupations, training and certification requirements, and academic curriculum preparatory requirements.*

It's also important to know the *job demographics* (which are the components of a job). These include the work conditions, environment, working hours, wages or salary paid, and whether or not the job will support your desired lifestyle.

Getting a complete profile before applying for a job will keep you from frequently changing jobs and being unhappy. So do your research! This guide discusses the most effective ways to get your questions answered.

In this phase of your life, you especially want to learn about entry level positions in the career fields and industries where you are interested in working. Start with informational interviewing.

Informational Interviewing

Interviewing interested, well-selected people can be a great way to get answers to your questions. This process provides opportunities for you to make direct contact with those already working in the job or career field of your choice. During those interviews, you can go directly to the source for answers to your career questions.

The benefits of conducting informational interviews:

◆ To get information that will help you make smart career choices

◆ To get accurate and current information about the industry, career field, salary, and job you are considering

◆ To get an understanding of a company, organization, and job structure

◆ To increase your knowledge of job duties and responsibilities

- ◆ To become knowledgeable about information that is useful for preparing your application and résumé

- ◆ To get advice on the direction of your academic curriculum, volunteer opportunities, and career choices

What to Know Before Conducting Informational Interviews

Doing informational interviews may require you to work outside of your comfort zone. However, the more you do them, the easier each one gets. You'll soon become relaxed as you discover that people generally enjoy talking about themselves and what they do.

For the most part, you'll find people helpful and happy to assist you. If you encounter rejection, don't take it personally; sometimes people with complex work schedules simply won't take extra time to stop and help you. Just keep focused and continue calling for appointments.

Remember, conducting informational interviews will build your confidence in knowing the match between yourself and the job. It will expand your knowledge of the job, provide the opportunity for you to meet interesting people, and give you access to current information. All of this can make a significant impact on the effectiveness of your job search and career choices. It can make the difference between finding an acceptable job and getting the job of your dreams. You may want to start with family members, neighbors, friends, and your parents for practice. It's worth stretching yourself. So get started!

I practiced my informational interview with my uncle. That experience really helped me.

Nikki

Things to Do

1. Call people directly if possible. Before calling, make sure you have the person's full name and exact job title. Emailing is an option that's not personable and therefore not as effective as calling. However, you can email if the person you're trying to contact already knows of you or has been referred to you.

2. Ask permission for their time before you proceed to engage in conversation. If necessary, make an appointment with them.

3. Explain the reason for your call. If someone else recommended you call, give that person's name.

4. Have paper and pencil handy so you can write down important things you want to remember as a result of the conversation.

5. Make sure you get the person's mailing address or e-mail address and *always* follow up with a thank you note.

Script for Conducting Informational Interviews

1. **Identify yourself.** "Hello. My name is _____. I'm a student at (state your school name). I'm doing some research on (state the job title or career of your interest)."

2. **Get the person's name and state the reason for your call.** "May I get the person's name who does (state job title or career interest)? Write down the person's name, and do not be embarrassed to ask for the correct spelling of the name. "I would like to conduct an informal telephone interview with (state their name) to gain insight about his/her occupation since it's a career path I'm interested in pursuing."

3. **Ask to speak with that person.** "May I speak with (state the person's name)?"
   If the receptionist will not put your call through, thank her/him and hang up. Write down the time and go to the next call. Call back later (wait at least one hour). When you call back, make sure you ask for the person by name. However, if your call gets through the first time, reintroduce yourself. Don't expect people to remember you until they get to know you.

4. **Begin the interview by greeting the person.**
   "Good (morning/afternoon) Mr./Ms. _____.
   May I have fifteen minutes of your time to ask a few questions about your career/job? I'm interested in (state job title or career field) and I'd like to know (state what you want to know)."

— or —

"Mr./Ms. _____, would you prefer we meet in person?"

If their preference is to meet with you, schedule a day and time that's convenient for that person. Be flexible. However, if you're given permission to proceed or sense it's alright, begin asking your questions. Be sure to have your questions ready.

5. **Close by expressing your appreciation.** Get a mailing address or e-mail address so you can send a thank-you note right away.

6. **Prepare and send a thank-you note.** Immediately following the informational interview, write and send a sincere note of appreciation.

Informational Interviewing Tips

1. Prepare a script and a list of questions before calling. This way, you'll present yourself as organized, serious, and prepared. People are more willing to help you when you are well prepared.

2. Correctly pronounce the person's name you are trying to reach, using the formal name (Mr. or Ms. Ball) or correct title (Dr. Ball or Judge Ball, etc.). Practice pronouncing it before calling; this will show you care enough to learn the person's title and status.

3. Speak clearly and confidently. It implies you know *exactly* what you want.

4. Stick to the time frame you've agreed upon to show respect for the person's time.

5. Have a pen and paper handy. This will help you keep calm, while also showing you're prepared to listen and take notes.

6. Ask for names of other people who might provide additional information. You will be surprised at the helpful responses you receive.

7. Don't give up too quickly. The more you practice, the easier the art of interviewing and being interviewed becomes.

Possible Questions to Ask

1. What skill, knowledge, or experience is required to qualify for your position?

2. What type of formal, specialized, or higher education does the position require?

3. What educational advice would you have for someone interested in your job or career field?

4. What other experience or training would be helpful for the job?

5. What types of volunteer work, internships, apprenticeships, or jobs did you do to prepare you for your career?

6. How did you get your first job in your chosen career path?

7. How would you describe your typical day at work?

8. What do you like most about your current job?

9. How much freedom and authority do you have in making key decisions?

10. Are there related fields you'd suggest I explore?

11. What is the starting salary for a position like this?

12. What are the possible career paths in your field of work?

13. Would you make the same career choice again? Why or why not?

14. If you could do it all over again, how would you change how you prepared for your chosen career?

15. Does this job/career allow you to be of service to others? Is it personally fulfilling?

16. What do you dislike about your current job?

17. What frustrates you about your job/career?

18. Do you work as a team member or independently?

19. What are your job-related goals? Where do you see yourself in the future in this job?

20. Where is most of your work done (inside or outside)? How would you describe your working conditions?

21. Do you offer a shadowing program? If so, may I shadow you for a day?

    Explanation: A "student shadowing program" is provided by many businesses to give you, the student, direct exposure to a job in a workplace setting. For a specified amount of time, you are partnered with an employee experienced in the position of interest and permitted to see how that person performs basic daily duties. You'll experience being in the environment along with seeing how employees interact. Once the program is completed, you'll have a better idea if this is the type of work you want to pursue.

22. What creative and innovative things have you done in your organization?

23. How did you acquire your current position?

24. What keeps you interested in your work?

25. Does your job require that you supervise or manage others?

26. What does it take to become successful in your job?

27. How is your job different than how it appears to an outsider?

28. Do you know anyone else I should or could talk with?

Reading

Reading is a valuable way to obtain information about a job or career field. The public library or your school career center should provide books, publications, directories, and articles filled with information on jobs, careers, and industry trends. Reading a variety of materials gives you different viewpoints and opinions.

You can also gather a wealth of useful information online. The resources listed here provide an excellent starting point.

American Almanac of Jobs & Salaries

Published by Avon Books, New York. Gives wages for specific occupations and job groups—including many professional and white-collar jobs. It also covers employment and wage trends.

Dictionary of Occupational Titles (DOT)

Published by the Department of Labor, this dictionary groups more than 20,000 jobs into major categories and describes the general requirements of each grouping.

The Occupational Information Network or O*Net replaces DOT. O*Net is a database of occupational requirements and worker attributes. It describes occupations in terms of the skills and knowledge required and how the work is performed. It also indicates typical work settings.

Directory of Directories

This lists directories alphabetically and also classifies directories according to subject.

Encyclopedia of Associations

This lists more than 22,000 professional, trade, and other non-profit organizations in the United States.

Guide for Occupational Exploration

Published by the Department of Labor, this groups the 20,000 jobs in the DOT under 12 general interest areas.

Occupational Outlook Handbook (OOH)

Published by the U.S. Department of Labor and Bureau of Labor Statistics, this outlines more than 300 kinds of jobs in terms of requirements, skills needed, types of employers, work conditions, and advancement potential. It also lists the 225 most popular jobs where 80 percent of all people work. The OOH is updated every two years.

Occupational Outlook Quarterly

Published by the U.S. Department of Labor, this provides an outlook for different sectors of the economy and individual occupations. It may contain featured articles on your particular selected job area.

O*Net Dictionary of Occupational Titles

Designed to update and replace the Dictionary of Occupational Titles (DOT), this describes 1,200 jobs held by nearly 100 percent of the workforce in the United States. It includes information on earnings, education, tasks, skills related to jobs, and much more.

Excellent Internet Sites

snagajob.com   www.snagajob.com
It helps locate part-time, temporary, and summer employment. The Job Seeker Resource Center offers assistance with preparing résumés and perfecting interviewing techniques. You can find job-hunting tips, post résumés, and get career questions answered.

summerjobs.com   www.summerjobs.com
It reviews nationwide summer job opportunities. You can take a free online career assessment, review job-hunting tips, and sign up to receive a career newsletter.

teens4hire www.teens4hire.org
It provides resources for teens interested in internships, employment, or work-based experiences.

youth@work www.eeoc.gov/youth
This website teaches about some of your rights and responsibilities as an employee.

myfirstpaycheck.com www.myfirstpaycheck.com
This hosts a job resource center and blog for teens.

teenjobsection.com www.teenjobsection.com
It helps teens find jobs. You can conduct your job search by state.

Researching helped me identify the exact job I wanted in the criminal justice career field after graduating from college.

I was able to narrow it down to a "Probation Officer" position. This position will prepare me for advancement opportunities in the career field.

David

Networking

Networking is the intentional exchange of knowledge, skills, information, resources, and/or contacts that are of immediate or future benefit to all parties involved. (*This networking definition was supplied by Kaye Cook.*)

Networking begins with people you have direct contact with and knowledge of.

Here's an example of networking: Ask a trusted teacher or someone you respect to recommend individuals you could contact to get your career questions answered. If your source grants your request and gives you leads, ask for permission to use the referring person's name *when you make contact.*

Networking is a way to get specific information that will help you make smart career choices. Through networking, you can gain knowledge not publicly known, get valuable leads, and broaden your contacts. It can be an excellent research tool.

However, don't begin networking until you have clearly defined your objectives.

Before You Network, Know...

✔ Your interests, skills, and abilities.

✔ The career fields your work-self closely matches.

✔ What questions you want to ask your contacts.

✔ What kinds of ways you wish the person to assist you.

✔ The best place to start networking, and then proceed to do so.

Your 30-Second Networking Commercial

Hello, my name is _____

_____. I am good at _____ and

_____.
(Your greatest interests)

I am interested in the career field of _____.
(Your career choice)

I could be good in this career because I like to do

_____, _____,

and _____.

Do you know of anyone interested in _____
(Same type of career choice)
who may help me with this career choice?

Networking Tips

◆ Know what information you want to gain from people you're networking with. In addition to showing respect for their time, it indicates you are well organized and prepared.

◆ Identify individuals you feel comfortable talking to and sharing with. Doing this immediately makes you feel comfortable expressing your thoughts.

◆ Organize your thoughts and questions so you present yourself as someone who knows exactly what he/she wants and gives the impression that you are committed. Be open to listen and learn from the recommendations presented to you.

◆ Ask your contacts for additional leads, such as recommendations for actions and suggestions for future contacts. You might be surprised how much this will increase your networking outreach.

◆ Get permission to use the referring person's name, if you sense that person is valued and respected. It can also encourage your prospective contact to open up and share information.

◆ Maintain records of your contacts, listing specific information about each. This way, you'll be able to keep track of the most important facts of your research for future use.

◆ Keep all appointments, agreements, and promises. Especially, keep personal and sensitive information about yourself and others confidential!

◆ Keep an open line of communication with your networking contacts that's *built on trust.* Be honest; people will appreciate that and will likely be more willing to help you.

◆ Always send thank-you notes. This simple act will show your appreciation and help keep you on their minds for future openings or endeavors.

◆ Continue to repeat the networking process until you have attained your goals. Don't be discouraged or afraid of hearing, "No." Continue to reach for your goals; eventually your persistence will pay off.

◆ Remember, networking is both giving and taking. When people help you, look for opportunities to help them in return.

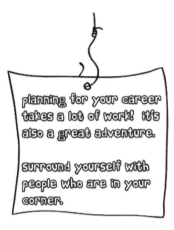

planning for your career takes a lot of work! it's also a great adventure.

surround yourself with people who are in your corner.

Networking Chart

Using the networking chart that follows will help you identify in advance individuals you think may have valuable information. It's designed to quicken your ability to pinpoint the best places and people to begin networking with.

Writing down your plans always makes it easier to act on your goals, keep track of your contacts, and identify the roles those contacts might play in your plans. That's the reason for doing a good job of completing this chart.

1. Family Members	2. Friends	3. Neighbors

4. Community Leaders	5. Church Members	6. Local Merchants

7. Online Contacts	8. Social Media	9. Twitter Followers

Career Fairs

Attending a career fair for the first time can be overwhelming. There, you'll meet representatives from many businesses who are ready and willing to talk with you. They will be fully prepared to answer your questions and ask several of their own. That's why it's important to prepare yourself for meeting and talking with a wide variety of employers.

You can go to your school counselor, local chamber of commerce, local colleges and universities, technical schools, and even the sponsoring company for information on local fairs in your area.

Also, you can search for career fairs in your area by visiting www.nationalcareerfairs.com. This site allows you to search for career fairs by city, state, and zip code.

Career Fair Preparation

At a career fair, your goal is gathering information that can help you make smart career choices. It's also an excellent way to have your questions answered. Employers are there to share information about their company, answer questions, and provide assistance that will increase your knowledge about the company. Ultimately, they want to recruit potential employees. The following are suggestions for getting prepared.

1. If possible, get a list of employers attending the fair. Often, you'll find the companies and businesses listed in the local newspaper or on the sponsor's website.

2. Familiarize yourself with each of your targeted employers' mission, product, and services by doing an online search. Then organize your thoughts and make a list of questions to ask each employer. Carry a notebook for storing handouts, pamphlets, flyers, and other materials received from employers.

3. Prepare a 60-second introduction (see 60-second Introduction template later in Chapter 2) and practice! Doing this will make you more comfortable and save time when you meet people.

Career Fair Do's

1. **Dress professionally.** First impressions last. Therefore, dress as if you were being interviewed for a job. Make sure your clothes are clean, carefully pressed, and neat. No excess jewelry, no baggy pants, no baseball caps. Make your appearance radiate "great potential" to a prospective employer.

2. **Be friendly.** Greet each employer with a smile and a firm handshake.

3. **Be prepared.** Have a list of questions to ask and a résumé to give to interested employers.

4. **Be independent.** Leave your friends at home. You want to appear mature, capable, and willing.

5. **Relax.** Be friendly and have a sense of humor. Be prepared to hold intelligent and interesting conversations. Maintain good posture. Look people in the eye when talking with them.

6. **Closure.** Close conversations by thanking the people for their time and leaving with a smile.

Career Fair Don'ts

1. **Don't be afraid to talk with employers.** They are attending the fair to talk with you and be helpful. This is the perfect time to get all of your questions answered.

2. **Don't use slang or negative words.** You don't want to leave a negative impression or show lack of respect and a poor attitude.

3. **Don't waste the employer's time.** Be articulate and get straight to the point. Have your thoughts mentally organized.

4. **Don't be impolite.** Wait your turn to speak. Don't invite yourself into another person's conversation. If you over-hear something interesting, listen and learn.

5. **Don't share your personal experiences with employers.** This is not the time to form lasting friendships. Allow your personal situation to remain just that—personal. Sharing private information can lead to wrong impressions. Remember, you want to get your career questions answered. Remain focused.

Your 60-Second Introduction

Hi, my name is _____.
                          (State your name)

I am a student at _____.
                          (Identify your school)

I am interested in _____.
                          (State the job title you are interested in)

Today, I'm gathering information that will help me make career choices.

I am interested in this type of work because _____

_____,

_____, and _____

_____.

(Share at least three reasons why you are interested in this particular career field.)

May I have a few minutes of your time to ask questions?

Questions you may want to ask:

1. Does your company have a student-hire or internship program for students with my skills and academic achievements?

2. Please explain what your company's career path is for my particular interest in _____.

3. What type of skills and educational requirements do you require for my particular area of interest?

4. What is the entry level position for the type of career I am interested in? _____

*Research is exploring today's
options that will lead to
tomorrow's possibilities.*

CHAPTER 3

The Employment Application Process

Nikki

Nikki

Nikki, 15 years old, is looking for summer employment. Because it's her first time completing an employment application, she wasn't sure how to properly complete it.

Nikki had many unanswered questions, such as:

◆ What are the requirements for a work permit?

◆ How should she describe her work experiences since she's never worked before?

◆ How would she locate current addresses and telephone numbers of individuals she has done various jobs for as a teenager?

For help, she visited the Career Resource Center in her local community center.

Nikki explained to the counselor there that she wants to earn money to pay for summer entertainment, save for upcoming school year events (e.g., prom, school dances, and sporting events), and pay for college application fees.

The counselor walked her step by step through the proper way to complete an employment application. Then she suggested Nikki download the free practice employment application package at www.newbeeginning.com.

Nikki felt more confident after the visit and set off to find more information on the recommended website. She completed and submitted the application to the manager of the local shopping center. Fortunately, she was hired on the spot!

Overview

The employment application is your tool to make a good first impression. You want the employer to know you have the skills, experience, and achievements to do the job you're applying for.

The employment application is the avenue you'll use to get that information to the employer. Your chances of making a good first impression on the application will improve by being aware of its appearance, content, and validity.

The employment application process is highly critical to your job search. It begins when you enter the employer's place of business to request an application and ends with the interview. The employment application links you with the employer as the first formal introduction. Remember, first impressions are based on the information listed on your application, as well as how you present it.

A good employment application will get you to that next step—the interview. Employers screen candidates based on the applications before the interviewing process begins.

How you complete the application tells the employer many things about you. For instance, leaving areas blank leaves the impression you didn't read the entire application. It may lead the employer to believe you'd rush through your work or not complete tasks or assignments.

Also avoid scratching out information when making a mistake. You don't want to leave a sloppy appearance. It may imply you are not a conscientious worker and that your work or appearance isn't important to you.

Tip: If there's not enough space in a block on your application form, use a clean sheet of paper and continue your answer. Be sure to list the block number your information refers to and attach the paper to your application.

Employment Application

Because both the *content* and *appearance* of your employment application determine if an employer gives you an interview, pay close attention to the information in this chapter.

The application typically covers four important points for the employer:

1. Who you are.
2. What your present or past work experience is.
3. What you can do and your potential for growth.
4. When you are available to start a job.

As a teen, you can demonstrate your experience and growth potential in a variety of ways. You have acquired skills and experience from home, school, church, and community service. Participation in sports and other organizations also shows many facets of your work-self as well as your ability to lead and be a valuable team player. Your aptitude for learning and growth will be portrayed by your current educational level and your future academic plans.

Many companies require you to complete their employment application because it is a legal document that can be upheld in court. Once you sign and date this application, you state, in effect, that everything on it is true. You can be fired from a job if it's found out you lied on the application.

You'll be required to complete many of your applications online, which means carefully proofreading your application. Be sure to attach any supporting documents requested, such as letters of recommendation, school transcripts, and references.

A behavior profile or questionnaire is sometimes part of the application process. This profile usually involves a series of questions about how you relate to others and how you might respond in a particular situation. As with the self-assessment, similar questions may appear in several areas of the question-naire with slightly different wording. The combined responses help establish your personality profile, so be honest and con-sistent with your responses.

Again, the application is the employer's first "look" at who you are. Make a good impression!

Personal Appearance

The application and your physical appearance reveal many things to the employer. When you walk into that company's place of business to pick up the employment application, people already begin to form opinions about you. They want to know who you are, how you heard about the job opening, whether you are qualified, and (most important) how you will fit in. They're sizing you up.

Specifically, impressions are formed based on how you are dressed, the way you talk, and even how you walk. Therefore, when picking up the employment application, be sure to dress appropriately. Give special attention to your personal hygiene. Use deodorant, and use perfumes and colognes conservatively. Cover or camouflage any tattoos. Wash and style your hair, and make sure your clothes are clean, neatly pressed, and suitable.

Remember, it's not appropriate to wear casual clothing such as baggy pants, t-shirts, mini-dresses, shorts, or sleeveless clothing. Any one of these things can create an unprofessional image.

What do you want to earn with your clothing? *Respect.* More than that, you want to be chosen on your skills, not turned away because of inappropriate clothing.

It's important to use proper English and absolutely no slang. Make sure the way you walk radiates confidence. Hold your head up high and be proud, give a firm handshake, and make direct eye contact. Ensure your completed application form is neat without scratch-outs or eraser marks. Don't fold or bend it.

All of these details create a representation of you on paper that's both pleasing to the eye and easy to read.

Content of the Application

Before you begin filling out the employment application, read it over. Then carefully follow the directions. Print neatly using an erasable black or blue pen; never leave any of the blocks blank. If a block does not apply to you, write "N/A" (not applicable). You do that to acknowledge you read that section so the employer won't think you intentionally left it blank or just overlooked it.

Use powerful action words to describe your skills and accomplishments. Action words also help you make a positive impression as you paint a clear picture of what you can do for the employer.

That means thinking in terms of how the employer thinks, which is the "what's in it for me?" question. Show your accomplishments along with the results and benefits of those accomplishments. Portray yourself as a problem solver who's eager to meet challenges.

Example of Power Word Usage:

Do not say or write on your application or résumé something like "I finished the following jobs …"

Do say or write, "My accomplishments are _____ which resulted in _____."

You can find sample word lists later in Chapter 3.

Validity of the Application

Never lie on the employment application; it is grounds for dismissal. More important, being dishonest is perceived as a character flaw.

When completing an employment application, *always* consider the big-picture effects. Think in terms of what you did, how you did it, and what you accomplished as it relates to the job you are applying for.

Also think in terms of how your skills and accomplishments can be re-invented in a way so that you can be of value in different jobs. This mindset will enable you to express in writing exactly what you want the employer to know about your skills, talents, and abilities. It will also help you conduct a successful interview.

You'll be able to provide a clear picture to the employer of what you can do for the company based on your skills and past experiences.

Keep in mind that as a teen, your past experiences can include many things besides formal work experience. Don't discount your experience as a team member, organization lead or participant, non-paid employee, babysitting, lawn care, and volunteer work.

Completing an Employment Application

Listed here are the common information blocks found on most applications.

Read each of them carefully; under each block is a description of the importance of the question and how you should answer.

Applicant Information
Block 1 – Last Name, First Name, Middle Initial
Pay attention to the order of the name block(s); the order often varies from application to application.

Block 2 – Date
List the present date if you are submitting the employment application immediately after completing it; otherwise, list the date you will submit it.

Block 3 – Street Address

List the address where you receive mail. If you have an apartment unit number, be sure to include it.

Block 4 – City, State, Zip

Spell these correctly and don't forget to list the zip code. Double check all of these for accuracy.

Block 5 – Phone

List the telephone number where you'll receive your messages. Make sure the area code is listed. If you have a cell phone (the norm for a teen), make sure your voice message sounds professional. Get rid of any long messages, radical music, and casual, offensive, or vulgar language.

Block 6 – E-mail Address

Be sure that your e-mail address is unique and has a professional tone. If you don't have one, create a free e-mail address on different websites (e.g., gmail, yahoo, and hotmail). Example: Sjohnson@yahoo.com.

Block 7 – Date Available

List "immediately" or an actual date. If you have a current employer, make sure you give a two-week notice, which is the standard minimum. Take this time to finish up work in progress, hand off projects, and be available to answer questions.

Also, know that the status of today's economy and job market has caused a new trend. Now, employees are giving a one-week notice to prevent from being passed over for a better opportunity.

Therefore, use your best judgment and, remember, you may need a reference from that employer, so make sure you leave on a positive note. Besides, you will show both new and old employers you are a person of good character—one who honors commitments and takes responsibility for your actions.

Block 8 – Social Security Number

Always have your social security card with you for filling out applications and as proof of identity when required. You'll use your social security number all of your life to keep track of your medical care and the employment taxes you pay into the social security system. It will also be used to calculate retirement, disability, and eligibility of death benefits due to you.

Do not guess; make certain the number you write on the application form is correct.

Block 9 – Desired Salary

List "open" or "negotiable" unless you're familiar with the salary range or wages paid for that job. Be realistic. Know the value of your skills and what employers are paying for them. Also know what the minimum wage is and become familiar with both commission and tip-based salary structures.

Block 10 – Position Applied for

Use the job title the employer used or what is listed on the source you are responding to (e.g., a job announcement, online or newspaper ad, bulletin, etc.).

Block 11 – Are you a citizen of the United States?

If not, list your employment authorization or resident alien card number that gives proof you are legally eligible to work in the United States. If in doubt, contact the U.S. Citizenship and Immigration Services.

Block 12 – Have you ever worked for this company?
Be honest. This gives your employer an opportunity to gather history and find out whether to rehire you. Your previous job performance may be the deciding factor used to determine any risk in hiring you.

Block 13 – Have you ever been convicted of a felony?
When this box is checked "yes," many employers then follow up during interviews or with criminal background checks to gather more information on the conviction. It's important to determine if it disqualifies you based on the specific requirements of the position you're applying for. Be sure to ask!

Education
Block 14 – Education (High School, Junior High, and Grammar School)
Correctly spell out the name of the school you attended and list the address. Always show month and year using double digits (example: 01/13) unless the format requires a different style. Answer the "did you graduate?" question by checking the appropriate block. In the degree block, list the correct title of what you earned (e.g., diploma, certificate, etc.).

Previous Employment
Block 15 – Employment History
Spell out the company's (or companies') full name; don't use abbreviations. List the current address and telephone number *including area code.*

List your previous supervisor's first and last names as well as your past job title. When listing a previous supervisor, use "Mr. or Ms."

Always show month and year using double digits. Make a positive statement when listing your reason for leaving. Describe your responsibilities using power or action words.

If you don't want the employer to contact your current employer, briefly explain your reason.

Foreign Languages
Block 16 – List any foreign languages you can speak, read, or write.

Your language skills may give you a competitive edge, so definitely list them, whether it's a job requirement or not.

Organizations
Block 17 – List membership in any professional or civic organization.

Having memberships in organizations demonstrates your leadership abilities and desire to cooperate with others as a team player. Be mindful to exclude those that may disclose your race, color, religion, or national origin if you believe they can impact you negatively.

Specialized Skills
Block 18 – List any specialized skills you have or equipment you operate.

Your specialized skills can give you the extra edge that lands you the job. Especially list those when the skill applies to the company's needs and enhances your skill set.

Disclaimer Signature
Block 19 – Disclaimer and Signature

Both are required because they provide disclaimers for dishonest answers and indicate the penalties in cases of intentional misstatements on the application form.

A signed application form provides authorization for the employer to conduct a background check and make the conditions of employment based on drug test results. Your signature is proof you understand the company's need to complete several more steps to move forward in the selection process.

Note: You'll find an example of an employment application on the following page. You can also download the employment application package at www.newbeeginning.com.

Sample Application Form

APPLICATION INFORMATION			
Last Name: BLOCK 1	First Name: BLOCK 1	M.I.	Date: BLOCK 2
Street Address: BLOCK 3			Apartment/Unit#
City: BLOCK 4	State: BLOCK 4		Zip: BLOCK 4
Telephone: BLOCK 5	E-mail Address: BLOCK 6		
Date Available: BLOCK 7	Social Security No.: BLOCK 8		Desired Salary: BLOCK 9
Position Applied For: BLOCK 10			

Are you a citizen of the United States? BLOCK 11	YES ☐ No ☐	If no, are you authorized to work in the United States? YES ☐ No ☐	
Have you ever worked for this company? BLOCK 12	YES ☐ No ☐	If so, when?	
Have you ever been convicted of a felony? BLOCK 13	YES ☐ No ☐	If yes, explain	

EDUCATION - BLOCK 14			
High School	Address:		
From: To:	Did you graduate? YES ☐ No ☐	Degree:	
Junior High	Address:		
From: To:	Did you graduate? YES ☐ No ☐	Degree:	
Grammar School	Address:		
From: To:	Did you graduate? YES ☐ No ☐	Degree:	

PREVIOUS EMPLOYMENT - BLOCK 15		
Company:	Telephone:	
Address:	Supervisor:	
Job Title:	Starting Salary:	Ending Salary:
Responsibilities:		
From: To:	Reason for Leaving:	
May we contact your previous supervisor for a reference? YES ☐ No ☐		

(Application form continued on next page)

PREVIOUS EMPLOYMENT - BLOCK 15

Company:		Telephone:	
Address:		Supervisor:	
Job Title:	Starting Salary:		Ending Salary:

Responsibilities:

From:	To:	Reason for Leaving:

May we contact your previous supervisor for a reference?   YES □   No □

PREVIOUS EMPLOYMENT - BLOCK 15

Company:		Telephone:	
Address:		Supervisor:	
Job Title:	Starting Salary:		Ending Salary:

Responsibilities:

From:	To:	Reason for Leaving:

May we contact your previous supervisor for a reference?   YES □   No □

List any foreign languages you can speak, read, or write. - BLOCK 16

	FLUENT	GOOD	FAIR
SPEAK			
READ			
WRITE			

Organizations: List membership in any professional or civic organizations. - BLOCK 17

Specialized Skills: List your specialized skills related to this position. - BLOCK 18

DISCLAIMER and SIGNATURE - BLOCK 19

I CERTIFY THAT THE INFORMATION GIVEN ON THE APPLICATION IS TRUE AND CORRECT. I UNDERSTAND THAT ANY FALSE INFORMATION, WILLFUL OR NEGLIGENT MISREPRESENTATION, OR FAILURE TO DISCLOSE ANY REQUESTED INFORMATION WILL CONSTITUTE SUFFICENT GROUNDS FOR TERMINATION OF EMPOYMENT WITHOUT NOTICE. I FURTHER UNDERSTAND AND AUTHORIZE THE COMPANY TO CONDUCT A PRE-EMPLOYMENT INVESTIGATION TO SECURE INFORMATION NECESSARY TO MAKE A DECISION BASED ON MY SUITABILITY FOR EMPLOYMENT. I FURTHER UNDERSTAND THAT YOUR COMPANY WILL ADHERE TO APPLICABLE STATE AND FEDERAL STATUTES CONCERNING THE SECURING OF INFORMATION, HANDLING, UTILIZATION, AND RELEASE OF INFORMATION OBTAINED IN THE PRE-EMPLOYMENT INVESTIGATION. IF THIS APPLICATION IS CONSIDERED FAVORABLY, I UNDERSTAND THAT I MAY HAVE TO PASS A PHYSICAL EXAMINATION AS A CONDITION OF EMPLOYMENT. I HEREBY UNDERSTAND AND ACKNOWLEDGE THAT ANY EMPLOYMENT RELATIONSHIP WITH THIS ORGANIZATION IS OF AN "AT WILL" NATURE, WHICH MEANS THAT THE EMPLOYEE MAY RESIGN AT ANY TIME AND THE EMPLOYER MAY DISCHARGE EMPLOYEE AT ANY TIME WITH OR WITHOUT CAUSE. IT IS FURTHER UNDERSTOOD THAT THIS "AT WILL" EMPLOYMENT RELATIONSHIP MAY NOT BE CHANGED BY ANY WRITTEN DOCUMENT OR BY CONDUCT UNLESS SUCH CHANGE IS SPECIFICALLY ACKNOWLEDGED IN WRITING BY AN AUTHORIZED EXECUTIVE OF THIS COMPANY. I UNDERSTAND IT IS THIS COMPANY'S POLICY NOT TO REFUSE TO HIRE A QUALIFIED INDIVIDUAL WITH A DISABILITY BECAUSE OF THAT PERSON'S NEED FOR A REASONABLE ACCOMMODATION AS REQUIRED BY THE ADA. I ALSO UNDERSTAND THAT IF I AM HIRED, I WILL BE REQUIRED TO PROVIDE PROOF OF IDENTITY AND LEGAL WORK AUTHORIZATION.

SIGNATURE: _____ DATE: _____

FOR PERSONNEL DEPARTMENT USE ONLY
Arrange Interview ☐ Yes ☐ No
Remarks_____

Carlos and Nikki

Carlos's and Nikki's thoughts and feelings are normal. It is common for job seekers to second guess and double check themselves after completing and submitting an employment application.

What's most important is that they took the first steps to securing employment by completing and submitting the applications.

They're both are on the path of finding the right job!

Verbs and Power Words

Use the action words below to fill out your employment application or résumé.

Remember, applications and résumés are tools used to introduce you to potential employers, so it's *critical* to do a good job of writing them. Using the wrong words or using a single word too many times can give the reader a negative impression.

It's worth taking the time to carefully construct your sentences. Your goal is to paint a creative picture of your work-self by describing the way you work and by giving the impression you are a bright, hardworking individual.

Challenge yourself to make your writing interesting to read. Review all lists carefully and keep in mind that, while there are headings for each category, the power words under the headings can be used to describe a variety of tasks and accomplishments. You'll want to get familiar with all the verbs and power words to broaden your vocabulary for describing your accomplishments.

Helping skills are used with people to get the job done: (Words with an asterisk [*] are also communication skills.)

Words	Meanings
Accomplish	*To complete or get the job done*
Adjust	*To modify or change*
Advise*	*To give suggestions or information*
Attend *	*To show up or appear*
Care*	*To give concerned attention*
Direct*	*To provide management advice*
Guide*	*To lead*
Led*	*Took the lead*
Listen*	*To pay attention*

Mentor*	*To guide someone*
Perceive*	*To understand*
Refer*	*To direct attention to*
Relate*	*To establish a connection*
Render*	*To give to another*
Service *	*To help or aid*
Speak*	*To express orally*
Teach	*To help someone learn*

Communication skills are used to communicate an idea or a point between two or more persons. They involve the qualities of listening, thinking, reasoning, and speaking:

Words	Meanings
Arrange	*To group in an organized manner*
Conflict resolution	*Working with others to resolve controversy, disagreements*
Critical thinking	*Using sound judgment and reasoning*
Customer service	*Providing assistance*
Edit	*To rewrite, correct*
Negotiate	*To arrive at the settlement of some matter*
Persuade	*To influence another's thoughts*
Present	*To formally share information*
Problem solve	*To find answers, solutions*
Proofread	*To check for errors*
Team building	*To bring together*

Detail skills involve working with processes or things of a simple to complex nature:

Words	Meanings
Approve	*To confirm*
Arrange	*To put in order, prepare, or plan*

Classify	*To arrange according to class*
Collate	*To arrange in order*
Collect	*To gather together*
Compile	*To put together*
Dispatch	*To send out*
Enforce	*To strengthen*
Execute	*To perform tasks according to instructions*
Facilitate	*To help bring about*
Implement	*To carry out*
Inspect	*To view closely*
Judge	*To form an opinion*
Operate	*To work*
Organize	*To arrange systematically*
Record	*To track*
Retrieve	*To recover or regain*
Tabulate	*To count, record, or list systematically*
Validate	*To confirm or prove*

Teaching skills are used to explain ideas, processes, and information so others can understand and apply:

Words	Meanings
Adapt	*To adjust*
Advise	*To suggest*
Compare	*To match*
Contrast	*To explore differences*
Develop	*To make better or to initiate*
Dialect	*Manner of expressing oneself*
Evaluate	*To determine worth or value*
Forecast	*To predict*
Interpret	*To explain the meaning of*
Knowledge	*Awareness*
Plan	*To prepare a detailed program*

Project	*To plan or estimate*
Research	*To collect information*
Teach	*To impart information*

Research skills are used to discover and analyze information:

Words	Meanings
Clarify	*To make easier to understand*
Collect	*To gather*
Critique	*To review*
Decide	*To make a decision*
Diagnose	*To recognize*
Gather	*To come together*
Interview	*To obtain information by conversing*
Investigate	*To closely examine*
Observe	*To take note of*
Recognize	*To admit or take notice of*
Review	*To view or see again*
Study	*To learn or memorize something*
Survey	*To examine as to condition, situation, or value*
Write	*To communicate by letter or written form*

Management skills are used to plan, organize (manage), and coordinate people, activities, and projects:

Words	Meanings
Administer	*To conduct*
Analyze	*To study in detail*
Assign	*To appoint as a duty*
Contract	*Binding agreement between two or more*
Control	*To have influence over*
Coordinate	*To bring into a common action*

Delegate	*To assign responsibility or authority to*
Direct	*To determine a course or direction*
Hire	*To employ*
Initiate	*To begin something*
Prioritize	*To rank in order*
Perform	*To carry out*
Produce	*To bring about*
Recommend	*To present as worthy*
Schedule	*To designate a fixed time*
Supervise	*To oversee*
Terminate	*To end*

Technical skills are used to perform complex tasks and to troubleshoot:

Words	Meanings
Assemble	*To bring together*
Communicate	*To make known*
Enable	*To provide the means*
Encourage	*To inspire*
Inform	*To communicate knowledge*
Instruct	*To give an order*
Stimulate	*To activate*

Financial skills are used to communicate monetary issues, problems, and solutions:

Words	Meanings
Allocate	*To assign*
Audit	*To check*
Bill	*An itemized list*
Budget	*To set aside money; a spending plan*
Calculate	*To determine by mathematical process*

Compute	*To figure*
Decrease	*To reduce*
Detail	*Extended attention*
Increase	*To add*
Inventory	*Itemized list of assets*
Maintain	*To keep*
Purchase	*To buy*
Solve	*To answer*

Manual skills are used to assemble and break down equipment following guidelines and regulations:

Words	Meanings
Bend	*To curve*
Bind	*To constrain*
Build	*To construct*
Drill	*To make holes*
Handle	*To have a grasp on the situation*
Lift	*To elevate*
Move	*To motion*
Operate	*To run*
Pull	*To draw*
Punch	*To stroke*

Creative skills are used to find solutions to problems or needs that are cost-effective, time-saving, and waste-reducing. They are also used to improve performance, generate ideas, or uncover hidden opportunities in problems:

Words	Meanings
Alter	*To change*
Ask	*To inquire*
Change	*To shift*

Create	*To originate*
Design	*To make an arrangement*
Generalize	*To make broad*
Listen	*To hear with attention*
Modify	*To change*
Paraphrase	*To repeat and rephrase*
Predict	*To guess*
Question	*To inquire*
Rearrange	*To sort*
Reconstruct	*To make over*
Regroup	*To reform*
Rename	*To change name*
Reorganize	*To redo*
Reorder	*To sort out*
Restate	*To reaffirm*
Revise	*To rework*
Rewrite	*To rephrase*
Simplify	*To make things easier*
Systematic	*Orderly*
Vary	*To differ*

Discriminative skills are used to determine the differences, strengths, and shortcomings of situations (useful for research and analytical tasks):

Words	**Meanings**
Choose	*To make a selection*
Collect	*To gather together*
Define	*To make distinct, clear, or detailed*
Describe	*To represent or give an account in words*
Detect	*To discover or determine the existence, presence, or fact*

Differentiate	*To define as distinct or different in character*
Discriminate	*To make a distinction*
Distinguish	*To define as separate*
Estimate	*To judge tentatively or approximately the value, worth, or significance of*
Identify	*To note the distinguishing character or personality of someone or something*
Isolate	*To set apart*
List	*To place words or numbers in a simple series*
Locate	*To set or establish in a particular spot*
Match	*To suitably associate a pair*
Omit	*To leave out*
Order	*The arrangement or sequence of objects*
Pick	*To select with care*
Place	*To appoint to a position*
Recognize	*To acknowledge acquaintance with*
Select	*To choose from a number or group by fitness or preference*
Separate	*To set or keep apart*

Laboratory skills are used in a learning environment:

Words	Meanings
Apply	*To put to use for a practical purpose*
Calibrate	*To adjust precisely for a particular function*
Compute	*To make calculations*
Conduct	*To direct the performance of*
Connect	*To become joined*
Convert	*To change from one form or function to another*

Demonstrate	*To show or prove the value of*
Feed	*To give food to*
Grow	*To increase in size*
Insert	*To put or thrust in*
Keep	*To stay in accord with*
Lengthen	*To increase the measure of a distance or dimension*
Manipulate	*To manage or utilize skillfully*
Plant	*To fit in place*
Prepare	*To get ready*
Remove	*To change the location position, station, or residence of*
Replace	*To put something new in the place of*
Report	*To make a detailed account or statement*
Reset	*To change the reading*
Set	*To fix by authority or appointment*
Specify	*To name or state explicitly or in detail*
Straighten	*To make straight*
Transfer	*To convey from one person, place, or situation to another*
Use	*The method or manner of employing or applying something*
Weigh	*To consider carefully*

Computer language skills are used when talking about computers and related subjects. They include:

Internet Providers
Telecommunications and cable companies are common internet service providers; check your local area.

Chat Groups or Rooms
IRC (Internet Relay Chat). internet online discussion between two or more people online and communicating together at the same time

Databases/Spreadsheets
Programs used to organize and to enter data, such as accounting or filing information

Download/Upload
Receiving or sending data over the Internet

DTP (Desktop Publishing)
Microsoft, Adobe, etc., have software programs used to create newsletters, magazines, books, flyers, etc. (including graphics)

Computer Programming
Creating programs to be used in a universal computer format

Electronic Mail (E-mail)
Communicating and sending messages locally or across the world through the internet

FTP (File Transfer Protocol)
File libraries or archives available to the public

Graphic/Art Programs
CorelDraw, Adobe Photoshop, etc., used to create art in various forms

Hardware
Monitor, keyboard, printer, mouse, etc.

Hypertext (HTML)
The programming language used on the World Wide Web (www)

Internet
Some of the most common uses are e-mail; IRC (Chat); www: FTP (file transfer protocol); conferencing (Net-meeting); news-groups (Usenet)

Presentation Programs
PowerPoint, HyperStudio, etc., used to create a computerized visual presentation of a particular subject

Search Engines
On the Internet: Yahoo, Alta Vista, Lyco, WebCrawler, Goggle, Bing, etc.

Software
Programs used to direct the operations of a computer

Websites
Individual sites presenting information to anyone who visits them; usually one site opens links to many others.

World Wide Web
A linking of web pages referred to as addresses or URLs (www)

Word Processing Programs
Microsoft Word, WordPerfect, etc., used to typeset and edit text and to do desktop publishing

Electronic language skills are used when talking about electronic devices:

Words	Meanings
iPad	*A tablet computer with a touchscreen interface that's smaller than a typical laptop but larger than the average smartphone.*
MAC address	*Short for Media Access Control address, a hardware address that uniquely identifies each node of a network*
IBM compatible	*A personal computer designed to function using the DOS operating system license by IBM*
iPhone	*An Apple internet-enabled smartphone that combines the features of a cellular phone, wireless internet device, PC tablet, and a digital camera*
Wi-fi	*A standard way computers connect to wireless networks*
Hotspot	*A site such as a coffee shop or other public establishment that offers Internet access over a wireless local area network linked to an internet service provider*
Android tablet	*A tablet computer that runs on the Android operating system and has most of the features of a PC*
Notebooks	*A portable computer that is smaller than a laptop*
Nook Tablet	*A tablet e-reader media player to download and read books on*

Kindle   *An electronic device for downloading, storing, and reading electronic books*

Sony reader   *A line of e-book readers developed by Sony*

Tips and Reminders

If you're asked to complete employment applications on the spot, make sure to come well prepared. Have available your social security number, current telephone numbers, and addresses. Write neatly and make certain all spelling is correct. It's wise to keep a notebook containing this pertinent information with you at all times. That allows you to take advantage of an unexpected opportunity.

To prepare, you can download the practice employment application package on www.newbeeginning.com/book-synopsis.html

Also complete the sample résumé in this chapter before you venture out. This will help you access the most current and accurate information, so you won't be guessing.

Refer to the power word listing in this chapter as you practice. You'll be surprised at how easily you can describe your qualities by writing in the active voice as well as using power words.

Go to apply for jobs alone; don't take friends or relatives to the offices with you. Be prepared, dress appropriately, and carry a black pen. Avoid embarrassment by knowing the current date so you won't put the wrong date on the application form. It's annoying for employers to be asked the date, and it gives the appearance you're not paying attention to detail. It clearly doesn't leave a professional impression.

While you complete the application form, it's wise to turn off your cell phone and allow your calls to go to your voicemail. Remember, getting that job is more important than answering a call or texting. People are watching what you do, and some of them may have influence in hiring you.

Follow-up Action

Be a proactive job seeker and always follow up after you've applied for a job. Make your initial follow-up contact with the hiring manager or company representative after the job application process has closed. If you're unsure of the closing date, then follow up within five business days from the time you submitted the application. You can make contact via telephone or e-mail.

Before you do, take time to do your homework. Before the follow-up contact, review your research notes so you'll have a working knowledge of the job itself and what the company does.

Be prepared to talk intelligently about them. Then share related qualities and experience about yourself that will give you a competitive edge.

When calling the company representative or hiring manager, start the conversation by stating your name, saying you submitted your application for the position, and asking if your employment package was received. If the person is someone other than the hiring manager, get the name, job title, and contact information of the person you're speaking with.

Next, ask about the timeline for the selection process. Having this information will make it easier for you to conduct your second follow-up, if necessary.

Assuming you're speaking to the person who can hire you, reiterate your interest and express your eagerness to talk about being a good match for the position. Let the manager know you're eager to come in for an interview.

Remember, don't appear desperate but do express excitement and initiative. Convey your gratitude for the opportunity to apply for the job. Throughout the conversation, use the name of the person you are speaking to.

It's probable you may have to follow up more than once. However, refrain from repeatedly making calls and sending numerous e-mails. If you receive a date to follow up a second time, stick to the timeline given.

It's appropriate to make your second follow-up within a week after the initial one. With this contact, your goal is to find out the status of your application and have your name recognized as a serious candidate. Always remain enthusiastic and positive without getting discouraged, especially if no status is available.

Continue with your job search, taking advantage of any other opportunities available to you. In the process, you'll learn the value of patience as well as the virtue of persistence.

Work Permit

The Fair Labor Standard Act (FLSA), also known as child labor laws, was enacted to protect your health, well-being, and educational opportunities. This law also covers age requirements and length of time a youth/teen can work. Work permits are required in 42 states. They are also known as "age certifications" or "employment certificates."

Some states require work permits only for teens under age 16, while others require permits for teens under 18. To learn about *your* state's requirements, talk with your school's guidance office and review your state labor laws.

Visit www.dol.gov/whd/childlabor.htm to learn information specific to your state. Pay attention to other state and federal labor standards that regulate hours, types of job, and working conditions for teen employees. Be an informed worker. It's important to your success!

You Can Do It!

Now that you've been given the tools to obtain the job of your choice, put those skills to use. Go forth to conquer that first job leading to your ideal career.

Remember, the jobs you're currently seeking are stepping stones. Your first few jobs are there to allow you to explore your career options. They also give you a way to save money for personal expenses and higher education (college or vocational school, or to help the family during challenging times.

Jobs You Can Apply For

- Administrative Assistant
- Amusement Ride Attendant
- Announcer
- Artist
- Athletic Coach for Youth Sport Teams
- Barber's Assistant
- Bagger
- Baseball Umpire for Little League
- Bookkeeping Clerk
- Camp Counselor for Youth
- Car Mechanic Helper
- Car Wash Attendant
- Carpenter Helper
- Cashier
- Childcare Worker
- Youth Coach
- Concession Stand Worker
- Cook (fast-food service)
- Computer Repairperson/Troubleshooter
- Dance Tutor
- Dishwasher
- Dog Walker
- Fast Food Worker
- Fitness Trainer for Youth

- Food Preparer
- Food Tester
- Golf Caddy
- Graphic Designer
- Hair Stylist Assistant
- Internships (public and private)
- Lawn Care Helper
- Lifeguard
- Music Tutor for Youth
- Painter's Assistant
- Paper Deliverer
- Park Ranger Assistant
- Pet Sitter
- Research Assistant
- Recreation Coordinator
- Restaurant Host/Hostess
- Retail Clerk
- Sales Associate
- Shampoo Clerk (Hair Dresser Assistant)
- Soccer Referee for Youth
- Social Media Planner/Coordinator
- Stock Clerk
- Ticket Taker
- Tutor
- Usher

- Veterinarian's Assistant
- Waiter/Waitress
- Web Page Designer
- Youth Advisor
- Youth Basketball Coordinator
- Youth Minister
- Youth Camp Assistant

So many options for me to explore...

I must assess my talents, skills, and abilities to determine a good match.

Job Application Checklist

Company Name:	Contact Person Name/ Phone No.:	Job Title:	Date Applied:	Follow-up Action:	Pending Action:	
						NOTES:

*Employment applications are
vehicles to get an employer's
attention; if used creatively,
unlimited opportunities will prevail.*

CHAPTER 4
Résumés

When preparing to write my resume, I must:

- Identify the job I'm writing the resume for
- Have a mindset to self-promote
- Be familiar with the industry jargon
- Think in an organized and logical manner
- Focus on my professional self not personal
- Write a cover letter to accompany my resume
- Write a reference sheet to have available
- Use a computer

Candiss

Candiss

Candiss is an 18 year old attending a non-traditional alternative program to get her high school diploma equivalency. Previously, life circumstances had caused her to drop out of school. This nontraditional program has given her a second chance to make things right for herself.

Candiss has come to understand that *"if it is to be, it is up to me."* She must redirect her energy to become a responsible, productive adult, and be as self-sufficient as she can.

Candiss completed life skills courses and is preparing to write her first résumé. She has logistically thought through the process and identified the most important aspects of the résumé-writing process.

After selecting the résumé format that best presented her skill-set to employers, she tailored the résumé to meet a specific employer's needs.

The employer was impressed with her résumé and asked Candiss to come back for an interview.

Overview

What is a résumé? A summary. You will write a résumé to *summarize* your high school courses, grades, academic and

community honors, extracurricular and sport activities, paid and unpaid work experience, and more. This summary, along with your soft skills, will help you present yourself favorably to an employer.

Soft skills are talents and personal attributes not acquired through formal training. Such attributes—being a good listener, having a positive attitude, showing integrity, and working well with others—give anyone the ability to perform well in a job or career.

The résumé and employment application have similar purposes—to apply for employment. At the beginning of your career journey, most employers require an employment application. But as you advance, having a résumé will be preferred.

You should prepare a résumé before you begin looking for work. The résumé will make completing an application much easier since your information will already be organized and well thought out. You'll be able to update it easily and have it readily available.

The best way to write a résumé is to write in a manner that represents you well. If you feel comfortable with the résumé you create, then you will feel confident in your job search.

The most creative aspect of résumé writing is selecting the proper format. The format depends on your targeted audience and the manner in which you want to present yourself.

The three basic types of résumé formats are: *chronological*, *functional*, and *combination*. Each has unique features and, when used appropriately, will serve to complement your professionalism, work experience, abilities, skills, and interests.

In short, your résumé is your marketing tool to catch an employer's attention.

Résumé Formats

Here is an introduction of the three résumé formats. Later in this chapter, you'll see more detailed information and samples of each format. Receiving this information early in your career journey will enable you to select the appropriate one as you advance.

Chronological Résumé:

A chronological résumé begins by listing your work history in reverse chronological order, with the most recent position listed first. This style works well for job seekers with a strong, solid work history.

Functional Résumé:

A functional résumé focuses on your skills and vast experience rather than your chronological work history and the company you performed the work for. It places more emphasis on your skills and achievements than work experience. It is most used by job seekers who have limited work experience but have education and related experience gained through avenues other than paid employment.

Combination Résumé:

A combination résumé lists your skills and experience first. Your employment history is listed in reverse chronological order. This format combines parts of both the chronological and functional format.

With this type of résumé, you can highlight skills relevant to the job you're applying for and list your work history. It is best used for job seekers who have good skills and may be transitioning to a different job or career field.

Can you select the format that will work best for you? Keep in mind that the *right* format will increase your chances of getting face-to-face interviews. For most teens, the functional format will serve you best because it allows the use of experiences from all areas of life. It will enable you to showcase noteworthy skills acquired through school projects and leadership roles, along with natural abilities and talents.

The use of *functional categories* to creatively describe your experiences and skills will present you more favorably to employers. They can easily see you have the requirements they're looking for.

You're probably asking, "What are the categories in functional résumés?" Good question.

They are categories that group activities or functions you have performed or learned. You can creatively show the variety of skills, talents, and knowledge you have by grouping them in categories such as:

> Administrative
> Artistic (hobbies, crafts, musical/dance/acting)
> Communication
> Computer Skills
> Customer Service
> Education
> Organizations/Affiliations
> Volunteer Experience

What Job Do You Want?

Before you can start writing your résumé, determine which jobs you both qualify for and care about. In today's job market, it is *crucial* to be specific. If you're not sure about the type of work you are interested in, review the results of your self-assessment. If you didn't take any self-assessment tests, think deeply about your likes and dislikes.

Your goal is to list the skills you enjoy using and match them to jobs that require those skills. Review the *Dictionary of Occupational Titles*, the *Occupational Outlook Handbook*, the website of targeted industries, help wanted ads, information you gathered at career fairs, and advice received from your networking contacts to help you.

Reviewing occupational titles and help wanted ads will actually spark you to consider job options you may not have thought of.

Thinking like a progressive, proactive person, do *not* limit your possibilities. You want to start gaining work experience and exposure to new and varied environments. Regard jobs in your early years as the building blocks of your ultimate life work and career.

Then, after identifying the type of work you want to do, select the résumé format that will best introduce you to employers.

Your Résumé is a Reflection of You

The résumé is your promotional piece. Use it as your calling card for introducing your unique skills and experiences. Accompanied by a cover letter, its purpose is to get you an interview.

However, résumé writing is not an exact science, so use these suggestions and examples as general guidelines, not a blueprint. As a general rule, when writing your résumé, include activities that relate to the job you're applying for and those that demonstrate your ability to do the job.

Remember, writing your résumé requires creative thinking and self-examination.

Getting Started

Start by listing your high school courses, grades, academic and community honors, extracurricular and sport activities, paid and unpaid work experience, and unique skills. You can build on this information by getting opinions from others about your qualities. Ask questions such as:

- What do others like best about me?
- What qualities do family members, teachers, and friends mention when they talk about me?
- What are my strengths? What are my weaknesses?
- Do I function best in a team setting or independently?
- What do others see as my biggest accomplishments?
- What are my unique talents, skills, and abilities?

At this point in the process, don't leave anything out. Write down whatever comes to mind. This is called "brainstorming," and the items you list are referred to as your *career profile*.

For accuracy, take time to review certificates, awards, report cards, position descriptions, school transcripts, and any other documents. They have valuable information about your background including dates, grades, titles, and names. Then list them in order of importance and dates. The process of *organizing* information will help when you decide where to place the items in your résumé.

Writing Your Résumé

Once your career profile is compiled and completed, you're ready to begin writing your résumé. Refer to the action verbs and power words in Chapter 3 to describe your experiences and communicate your skills. Next, let's examine various headings you can put on your résumé and the type of information to be included under each.

Highlights of Qualification

You may wish to use this heading—Highlights of Qualification—near the top of the page to get the reader's attention.

This heading is used when sharing personal and professional traits you believe will help you stand out as the best candidate. It includes items such as language proficiency, special training, awards, and security clearances. *Note: Security clearances are required for many government jobs.*

Normally, three to five short statements are listed. The information in the body of your résumé must support these statements. First, list the most important responsibilities, which are things directly related to the job you're applying for. *This is a strategy that may give you a competitive edge.*

Example:

- ◆ Fluent in Spanish and French
- ◆ Proficient in Point of Sales terminals
- ◆ Strong customer service/communication skills.
- ◆ Recipient of the "Team Star Award"
- ◆ Able to persuade and influence people to take action.

Personal Heading

This heading is located at the top of the page and should include *your complete formal name, address, telephone number, and e-mail address.* Avoid nicknames and be sure your e-mail address is professional. List only one telephone number and address to conserve space. Make sure your name stands out by using bold letters or a larger font size.

Example: **Sophia Johnson**
123 Local Drive
Peaceful, Ohio 45678
Phone Number: 000-100-1000
E-mail Address: name@e-mailaddress.com

Career Objective

Although including your career objective is optional, it's highly recommended because it tells the employer immediately what you're looking for.

Make your career objective statement employer-centered, clear, and concise. If you know the exact job title used by the employer, you can list it as your career objective. Focusing on aligning your career objective with the employer's requirements.

Remember, employers are interested in what you can do for them, not what they can do for you.

Examples of employer-centered career objectives are:
- A Cashier Position
  You used the job title listed on the job announcement.

- Cashier position requiring sales, customer service, and accounts payable/receivable skills.
  You read the job announcement and saw that the employer needs a cashier with skills in sales, customer service, and accounts payable and receivable. You have the related experience using these skills. So you let the employer know your skills match the job requirement.

- Position as a Cashier for My General Shopping Center
  You know you want a cashier position at My General Shopping Center and that My General Shopping Center has cashier position openings.

Work Experience

This heading can be titled as your Work Experience, Employment Information, or Summary of Relevant Skills and Experience. The one you choose depends on your preference and particular situation.

Usually, the work experience area comes next on your résumé. However, at times you may want to list your education before your work experience. Some employers value education equal to or more important than work experience. As a teen, your education will likely be more prominent than your work experience.

Training

This is optional. However, if you have completed a type of formal training directly related to the position you are applying for, then include it on your résumé. List the most recent training first.

Education

This category is particularly important if you're expecting your educational experience to qualify you for the job. List your major field of studies, grade point average (GPA), and any courses directly related to the field of work you are applying for. Your education will weigh heavily in the employer's eyes, so list it in a way that presents you well.

Example:

East High School – Peaceful, Ohio 67892
Major: Vocational Studies; GPA: 3.0
Related Courses: Accounting I & II; Grade: A
Business Math; Grade: A

Courses

If you list specific courses, make sure they're related to the job or industry you're applying for. The courses you list should be important to the employer's business or show a special academic focus.

Example:
Career Objective: A Student Research Intern, in the Research Unit at the International Economics Agency.

Related Courses:

HST 102:   World History; Grade: A
HST 203:   Modern World Studies; Grade: A

GPA

Some employers show a lot of interest in your grades, while others don't. Deciding to include your GPA on your résumé depends on your past performance.

Keep in mind your desire to present your accomplishments in the best possible light. Your GPA is an educational accomplishment. There isn't a rule saying that only your overall GPA can be placed on your résumé. Feel free to list your GPA in different ways if it improves your presentation. Be honest with how you came to any of your conclusions; the grades you list should agree with official records.

Example:

GPA: 3.0 in general studies
GPA: 3.5 /4.0 previous semester
GPA: 4.0 in business classes

Note: A specific GPA may be a requirement to qualify for certain internships and student-hire employment positions. Again, present your grades in the best light possible.

Work History

Under this heading, include start and ending dates, position title, and the employer's name and location for each job held. List your current or most recent job first and work backwards from there.

An example of how to list your work history follows.

Work history example:

Jan 2013–Present	Cashier My General Shopping Center 12345 Friendly Lane Peaceful, Ohio 67890
Jan 2012–Jan 2013	Movie Ticket Taker Local Movie Theater 678 Cheerful Drive Peaceful, Ohio 23456
Jan 2011–Jan 2012	Fast Food Worker Fast Food Restaurant 901 Merry Street Peaceful, Ohio 78901

Optional Headings

The next categories are optional headings you could use to make your résumé more appealing.

Extracurricular Activities

List the various activities you participated in to show the many facets of acquired and soft skills you have obtained. List successes in extracurricular activities that demonstrate your abilities.

Skills

List the skills most relevant to the position. You may also list strong supporting skills that show your potential.

Honors and Awards

List honors and awards that present a fuller picture of your strengths. Provide titles and dates won of your awards.

Carlos, Nikki, and Chris are brainstorming their approach to start writing their résumés.

The assistance Nikki received from the counselor on completing employment applications helped her better understand the résumé-writing process. She shares with them important information to consider.

Nikki is "paying it forward" by helping her friends this way.

Choosing a Format

You've been introduced to the three types of *résumé formats*, but which format best suits your situation?

The résumé format refers to the way content is organized. When choosing, it's important to select the one that will best show off your skills and experience to the employer. Your selection will depend on your career goals, accomplishments, and fit for the employer's needs.

The following pages contain descriptions and samples of the three basic types of résumés.

The Chronological Résumé

The *chronological résumé* features a traditional structure that's most familiar to employers. It focuses on your experience. Begin by listing your current or most recent job first. Give the job title, a detailed description of your duties and responsibilities, and the company's name and address.

This structure is primarily used when you remain in the same type of work or have been steadily employed for a number of years. It shows advancement in a career field and includes impressive titles of previous jobs. It also directly communicates your purpose, past achievements, and probable future performance.

If you have work experience in the field you're applying for and your job titles show progress, this format is recommend. However, it won't work well for teens looking for their first jobs, nor for anyone with a patchy work history—someone who changes jobs or career fields frequently. Once you have a steadier work history and are looking for similar jobs, you may wish to change to this format.

Advantages

The chronological résumé may appeal to older, more traditional employers and becomes the best choice for jobs in conservative fields. This format makes it easy for the hiring manager to see what you accomplished in previous jobs.

The chronological résumé format:
- Showcases growth in skills and responsibility.
- Shows off promotions and impressive job titles.
- Can indicate loyalty to an employer.

Disadvantages
Because it can be difficult to highlight what you do best, this format is rarely appropriate for teens looking for their first job, making a career change, or entering a new field. It might:
- Emphasize gaps in employment.
- Highlight frequent job changes.
- Emphasize employment but not skill development.
- Show lack of related experiences and career changes.
- Point out demotions and career setbacks.

It's best used by teens who have:
- A steady work record.
- Experience that relates directly to the position they are applying for.
- A strong, solid work history related to the job and industry.
- Impressive, well-known companies as ex-employers.

Overall, by listing your most recent work experience first, this style provides a comprehensive summary of your work history, education, and accomplishments in reverse chronology. Be sure to provide clear job titles, employer/company names, and dates of employment.

A sample of the chronological résumé follows.

Sample Chronological Résumé

Sophia Johnson
123 Local Drive
Peaceful, Ohio 45678
Telephone number: 000-100-1000
E-mail Address: name@e-mailaddress.com

Objective:	A Cashier Position
Education:	East High School, Peaceful, Ohio 45679 Major: Vocational Sales G.P.A.: 3.0/4.0 in business courses
Work Experience: Jan 2013-Present	Cashier My General Shopping Center 12345 Friendly Lane Peaceful, Ohio 67890
	Greet and assist customers. Process cash, checks, and credit card transactions. Count money to verify amounts and issue receipts for funds received. Issue change and process checks for purchases. Compare total cash register receipts with the amount of currency in register to verify balances.
Jan 2012–Jan 2013	Movie Ticket Taker Local Movie Theater 678 Cheerful Drive Peaceful, Ohio 23456
	Greeted and assisted patrons at Movie Theater and distributed marketing materials. Collected admission tickets and passes. Examined tickets and passes to verify authenticity. Seated patrons, searched for lost articles, and directed patrons to restrooms and telephone facilities. Monitored patrons' activities to prevent disorderly conduct and rowdiness. Served patrons at refreshment stand. Changed advertising displays.
Special Activities: Jan 2012–Present	Class President and active member of Vocational Sales Club

The Functional Résumé

The functional résumé highlights and organizes your skills, accomplishments, interests, and strengths to support your career objective by grouping them into categories.

This format enables the reader to see immediately what you can do without reading the entire résumé. The reader then has the luxury to scan the résumé by reviewing the categories listed. It also helps an employer make a faster hiring decision based on seeing skill areas that highlight your aptitude and potential.

Advantages

The functional résumé will help you jumpstart your employment history or reach for a new career goal or direction. This format is highly recommended for teens with minimal work experience. It supports highlighting your educational experience and skills acquired through areas of your life such as school activities, volunteer work, academic projects, athletic involvement, recreational activities, classroom work, and projects done in social and civic organizations.

The functional résumé format:

- Emphasizes skills rather than work history; it allows the writer to focus on relevant experience.
- Organizes a variety of experience (paid and unpaid, and other activities).
- Disguises gaps in work history or a series of short-term jobs.
- Makes it easier to target the résumé (relate your experience to the job).

Disadvantages

This format does not reveal what the applicant did in each job, the employer name, or job titles. That may be viewed negatively by conservative interviewers. It can:

- Be viewed with suspicion by employers due to lack of information about specific employers and dates.
- De-emphasize growth/job titles.
- Fail to connect skills/accomplishments with specific situations in the case of multiple jobs.
- Require extensive background work or knowledge of job/employer.

It's best used by teens who have:

- Limited or no work experience.
- Gaps in employment.
- Developed skills from volunteer experiences and other areas that will help them qualify.
- Frequently changed jobs.

A sample of the functional résumé follows.

Sample Functional Résumé

Sumsing Wong
001 Aladdin Way
San Francisco, California 90001
Telephone Number: 000-100-0000
E-mail Address: name@e-mailaddress.com

Objective: A Cashier position requiring sales, customer service, and accounts payable/receivable skills.

Sales
- Sold men's and boys' outer garments.
- Advised customer of styles and appropriateness of garments for various occasions.
- Operated cash register to complete sales transactions.
- Opened and closed cash drawers.
- Balanced daily cash transactions. Accomplishment: Named Employee of the Year for balancing all transactions at the end of the day for cash reconciliation.

Customer Service
- Greeted and assisted customers.
- Researched customer complaints and conducted follow up.
- Accomplishment: Recipient of the Star Performance Award based on customer feedback for providing excellent service.
- Advised customers of current sales and promotional opportunities.
- Referred customers to appropriate sources for assistance.

Accounts Payable/Receivable
- Compiled and posted general ledgers.
- Calculated interest and added charges.
- Reconciled and balanced accounts.

Education: Ronald Reagan High School,
San Francisco, California 00001
Major: Vocational Studies, GPA: 3.0/4.0
Related Courses:
Accounting I & II, Grade: A
Business Math, Grade: A

Special Honors and Activities:
Recipient of Chamber of Commerce Youth Business Award, 2012.
Served as Distributive Educational Secretary for Class of 2012.

The Combination Résumé

The combination résumé includes elements of the chronological and the functional formats. This format may be exactly what you need if you want to enter into a new career field with minimum transferable skills.

To best show your qualifications, be sure to stress your accomplishments and skills, and include your work history. This is the perfect résumé for someone with work experience who wishes to change to a job in a related career field. It's also good for a teen looking for education and work experience to qualify him or her for the job.

Advantages

The combination résumé maximizes the advantages of both formats—chronological and functional. It will:

- Highlight most relevant skills and accomplishments.
- De-emphasize employment history in less relevant jobs.
- Combine skills developed in a variety of jobs or other activities.
- Minimize drawbacks such as employment gaps and absence of directly related experience.

Disadvantages

This format tends to be longer than the other two. Information could be repetitious if listed in both the functional areas and work history section.

It's best not to list detailed descriptions in the work history section. Only the basic information is needed. Simply tell the reader the places where you previously worked, including the job title, company name, address, and dates employed. It can:

- Be confusing if it's not well organized.
- Require more effort and creativity to prepare.

It's best used by teens who:

- Desire to use education and work experience to qualify them for the job.
- Want to emphasize soft skills and personal qualities such as initiative, dependability, good customer service, etc.
- Aim to show their ability to grow with a job.
- Frequently change careers or in transition to a new and different career field.

A sample of the combination résumé follows.

Sample Combination Résumé

David Crockett
000 Bambi Lane
Miami, Florida 00000
Telephone No.: 000-111-1111
E-mail: name@e-mailaddress.net

Objective: Position as a Sales Associate for Dani J Couture.

Education:
>Miami Dade High School
>Miami, Florida 00001
>Major: Vocational Studies, GPA: 3.0
>Related Courses: Accounting I & II, Grade: A
>Business Math: GPA: A

Highlights of Qualifications:
- Fluent in speaking, reading, and writing Spanish and French.
- Proficient in using Point of Sales (POS) terminals.
- Knowledgeable of accounts payable/receivable postings techniques.
- Able to work with a diverse group of people.

Sales
- Sold outer garments for men and boys.
- Advised customers of styles and appropriateness of garments for special occasions.
- Operated the cash register to complete sales transactions. Opened and closed cash drawers.
- Balanced daily cash transactions.

Customer Service
- Greeted and assisted customers.
- Researched customer complaints and conducted follow up. Advised customers of current sales and promotional opportunities.
- Referred customers to appropriate sources for assistance with purchase specials and sales.
- Maintained customer accounts payable/receivable. Performed calculations and posted general ledgers.
- Computed interest and added charges.
- Reconciled and balanced accounts.

Work History

Cashier	My General Shopping Center 12345 Friendly Lane Peaceful, Ohio 67890	Jan 2013–Present
Movie Ticket Taker	Movie Ticket Taker Local Movie Theater 678 Cheerful Drive Peaceful, Ohio 23456	Jan 2012–Jan 2013

Résumé Guidelines

The following are general guidelines for writing your résumé. The information may vary slightly according to profession, situation, or geographical location.

Résumé Essentials

- Length should be limited to one page but not to exceed two pages.
- Make margins (top, bottom, left, and right) approximately one inch.
- Leave plenty of white space to be easy to read: 50 percent white space and 50 percent print.
- Font size should be no larger than 12 point but no smaller than 10 point. Use conservative (not contemporary) font styles such as Times New Roman, Helvetica, or Arial.
- Align justification to the left.
- Use black ink.
- Make layout easy to follow and information easy to locate.
- Make it appear neat, clean, and error free.
- Weight of paper should be 20- to 25-pound bond, rag or linen, and a neutral color.
- Envelope and cover-letter paper should match résumé paper.

Résumé Content

- Show responsibility and results relating to the needs of the company.
- Give examples of accomplishments and the ability to solve problems.
- Show statistics and numbers.
- Be honest, positive, and specific.

- Use category headings: objective, work experience, education, training, honors, and awards. This will make your résumé more pleasing to read.
- Avoid being wordy and using abbreviations. Use action verbs and be brief.
- Include volunteer experience, language proficiency, internships, and certificates that relate to the position.
- Research the company and know what information would impress the decision-makers.
- Use industry terminology.
- Be accurate with your information and make sure you use correct spelling and grammar.

General Tips

- Write your own résumé. Do not hire a résumé writing service. It is costly and may seem insincere. Normally, these services do not customize the résumé so the writing appears mass produced. The résumé doesn't highlight the individual experience. It's easy for an employer to spot these résumés. And it's difficult for the individual to speak intelligently at the interview because he or she didn't create it.
- Have a family member or friend proofread your résumé.
- Do not mass mail résumés.
- Customize your résumé to match the job you're applying for.
- Use your résumé to prepare what to say during the interview.
- Use a computer to produce your résumé. If you don't have a computer, go to copy centers, libraries, schools, or local job service centers.
- Take extra copies of your résumé when you job search or go on an interview. It's possible you could interview with more than one person while you're there.

◆ Never provide names of references on your résumé. Either enclose a reference sheet or provide references when requested.

Writing a Federal Résumé

The writing style and information included in a résumé for a federal government job differs from a private-sector résumé. Federal employment laws and rules require you to use a different approach.

The government's objective is to provide everyone who applies for federal employment an equal opportunity to access it. The federal government requires certain information that the private sector does not require.

That information could include:

◆ Social security number
◆ Job announcement number of the job you're applying for
◆ Address and telephone number of schools attended
◆ Address and telephone number of sources listed on your résumé where you gained paid and non-paid experience
◆ Number of hours worked
◆ Awards earned
◆ Language skills
◆ Special training

Gather this information and supporting documents well in advance to ensure you have the most accurate and complete material. Having federal employment experience may increase your future career options. Summer employment with the federal government and internships should be considered for that reason. You'll be exposed to a challenging work environment and afforded the opportunity to learn and grow. It's a great way to gain marketable skills, develop your work ethic while earning money, and start building a professional network.

Federal employees are civil service members. Most of them adhere to standards that are viewed in a positive manner by employers. A security background check is necessary to obtain the required level of security clearance. Therefore, having federal experience will most likely give you a competitive edge over those who don't have federal jobs or internships.

USAJOBS. The official site to visit is www.usajobs.gov. There, you'll find a tutorial and many helpful resources to guide you.

Once you create your USAJOBS account, you'll be able to store up to five different résumés used to apply for federal employment. You can also make a résumé searchable to allow agencies to find you. I highly recommend you visit this site and navigate through the tutorial program to learn how to use its features.

Applying for a federal government job is a three-step process: 1) create your account, 2) search for jobs, and 3) manage your career.

Note: You don't need an account to search for jobs, but you have to establish an account to *apply for* jobs.

USAJOBS contains a wealth of information. The site can help you get familiar with government terms. The postings for employment opportunities are called job or vacancy announcements. Read them thoroughly and pay attention to the requirements for qualifying for the job. Also, the job titles for government jobs are different than private sector. Become familiar with what's called Standard Occupational Codes that group jobs into series.

There may also be a questionnaire used to screen and rate candidates as to their competency level. The tool, called an Occupational Questionnaire, consists of multiple choice and yes/no questions to glean information about a candidate's competency and skills.

In addition to spending time on USAJOBS, also visit the U.S. Office of Personnel Management website for additional resources at www.opm.gov.

Student Programs. The federal student programs are titled the Pathways Program for students in high school, college, trade schools, and other qualifying educational institutions. Under this program, you will see job announcements for paid opportunities to work in agencies while completing your education. The Pathways Program offers summer employment and internships for students ranging from high school through post-graduate schools. You must be 16 years old to apply for the federal government summer employment program.

Visit www.opm.gov/Hiring Reform/Pathways/ for details and the most current information for your geographical area. In addition to visiting USAJOBS, go to specific government agencies' websites to view employment opportunities.

You may have other federal employment options in your area, such as volunteer programs, shadowing programs, and part-time or intermittent employment opportunities. As you advance through your career journey, you'll find that federal employment options will increase.

Another option available to you is the "Take Your Child to Work Day". You can go to work with a federal employee to learn about what that person does and how the department operates.

Do your research before writing your federal résumé. Strive to understand the hiring process for the federal agencies or departments you're applying to. It will be helpful to know in advance the preferred application form, the opening and closing dates for accepting summer hire applications, and the process for submitting supporting documentation.

Knowing in advance about the agency that interests you will increase your chances of being properly prepared. As a result, you will receive more considerations for employment.

After you complete your federal résumé, use it as your master for preparing future résumés. You can search for jobs by location, job category, and agency.

In summary, to apply for federal employment, place your résumé in USAJOBS, the government's official job website, or apply online at a specific government agency website.

The USAJOBS website provides access to more than 30,000 job listings daily as well as job announcements, various forms, and employment fact sheets. Job postings, updated hourly, are available to job seekers in a variety of formats. This ensures accessibility for those with differing physical and technological capabilities.

State and Local Government

As with the federal government, be sure to research and access your state and local government agencies to seek employment opportunities. You can find summer and student hire programs at these levels as well.

A sample of the federal résumé follows.

Sample Federal Résumé Format

Carlos Mendoza
SSN#: 000-00-0000
Candidate Source: External, DEU
1234 Local Street Road
My City, State 00000
Job Title: Cashier
Job Announcement No.: 2012-HQD-0123
Cell Phone No.: 000.000.0000
Home Phone No.: 000.000.0000
E-mail: name@e-mailaddress.net

Summary of Skills: Sales, Customer Service, Accounts Payable, and Accounts Receivable. *(Document the duties performed to show how you used these skills in the experience section.)*

Experience: *(Be descriptive in explaining the duties you performed. List the duties related to the type of job you're applying for. You want to show that you have transferable skills. For strong writing, refer to the active verbs and power words in Chapter 3.)*

1 Jan 2013 – Present, 20 hrs. per week, Cashier, ABC Company, 12345 Friendly Lane, San Antonio, Texas, 00000, Immediate Supervisor: Mr. Smith, 000.000.0000.

I greet and assist customers with making purchases for goods and services in a convenience store. Make change, cash checks, and issue receipts to customers. Open and close points of sales terminals, balance accounts payable and receivable, and reconcile and balance accounts. Research customer complaints, conduct follow up, and refer disputes claims to supervisory personnel for resolution. Advise customers of current sales and promotional opportunities. Compute interest and add charges. ACCOMPLISHMENT: Maintain a 100% accuracy rate for balancing transaction records.

1 Jan 2012 – 1 Jan 2013, 20 hrs. per week, Cash Clerk, DEF Company, 6789 Associate Drive, San Antonio, Texas, 00000, Immediate Supervisor:
Ms. Jones, 000.000.0000

I operated cash registers to complete sales transactions for a grocery store. Opened and closed cash drawers and balanced cash transactions. Sold lottery tickets and other goods to customers. Resolved customers' complaints and elevated issues to the proper personnel as required. Bagged, boxed, and wrapped merchandise. Stocked shelves, marked prices on items, and cleaned facilities. ACCOMPLISHMENT: Resolved 95% of complaints without supervisory personnel.

EDUCATION:
T.J. Holmes High School, San Antonio, Texas 00000, Major: Vocational Studies, GPA: 3.0

EDUCATIONAL COURSE WORK:
Accounting I & II – Grade: A
Business Math – Grade: A

SPECIALIZED TRAINING: Summer Safety for Teen Worker, May 2013

LICENSES/CERTIFICATES: First Aid/CPR/AED

AWARDS: Honor Roll, June 2012

LANGUAGE SKILLS: Spanish, Fluent

TRAINING: Typing I and II

Writing a Cover Letter

The cover letter plays an important role in the job search process. It adds a personal touch to your résumé and shows employers you're a serious and professional applicant.

When done properly, your cover letter can increase your chances of getting an interview and strengthen your ability to compete for jobs. A well-written cover letter demonstrates your communication and organizational skills and shows that you are the type of person who is willing to go the extra mile.

Your cover letter can give you another edge over other applicants because it describes how your specific skills and accomplishments uniquely qualify you for the job.

3 Basic Techniques for Writing a Cover Letter

1. **Tailor it to fit the employer's requirements:** Before you start the writing process, review the criteria for the position and make a list of what the employer wants. It may include specific areas of expertise, technical knowledge, transferable skills, and/or personality traits. Put those items in your letter to demonstrate you have the desired qualifications. Creatively describe in the letter how you can meet the employer's needs.

2. **Market yourself:** Tell the employer why you should be hired. Be assertive about your qualifications but not egotistic. Make the tone of your letter professional, yet personable. One of the best ways to judge your letter is to read it out loud. Make sure you're not tripping over any of your words. Revise it until it flows naturally and has a conversational tone.

3. **Keep it simple**: You have many options for formatting this letter. If you're unsure, review business books or get advice from a business teacher. Format the letter as a business letter. Use the simple block format with left flush margins (refer to the sample letter later in this chapter). Limit it to one page (three-to-five paragraphs) with one-inch margins all around.

Letter Content

First Paragraph: In your introductory paragraph, your objective is to get the reader's attention and describe the position you're interested in.

Example:
In response to your advertisement posted in the front window for a cashier position, I have enclosed my résumé for your review.

— or —

Your recent advertisement for a cashier's position caught my attention, as my qualifications appear to be compatible with your requirements.

— or —

I was referred by...

Second Paragraph: This paragraph is the body of your cover letter. It's where you outline your qualifications for the position—those that make you the best candidate for the job. Focus on the most relevant aspects of your background such as experience, course work, grade-point average, and your personal and professional traits. Do *not* repeat what's in your résumé. Instead, include information that will catch the employer's attention and compel him/her to read your résumé.

Example:
My two years of progressive retail experience qualifies me as the best candidate for your position. As specified in your ad, I am skilled in sales, customer service, and accounting. In addition, I am the current recipient of the YMCA Youth Community Award. After reviewing my résumé you will see my qualifications are a perfect match for your cashier position.

— or —

My qualifications for the position include the completion of a two-year business course requirement at East High School in Peaceful, Ohio. I completed the course work with a GPA of 3.8 and currently hold the highest honor award titled Business Student of the Year. I am skilled in sales, customer service, and accounting.

Third Paragraph: In the closing paragraph, request a meeting or personal interview. Mention that you look forward to hearing from an interviewer. State how you can be reached. Thank the employer for taking time to consider your application.

Example:
I look forward to meeting with you to discuss my qualifications and your job opportunity in detail. I will call on Monday, January 10, 2013, to schedule a convenient time to meet with you. Thank you for your time.

— or —

I believe I can make a positive contribution to the Fine Food Store and look forward to discussing my capabilities in detail. I am available for a personal interview at your earliest convenience and may be reached after 5 p.m. at the telephone number or e-mail address listed on my résumé. Thank you for your consideration.

A sample cover letter follows.

Sample Cover Letter

January 6, 2013

Mr. Brian Ball, Owner
Fine Food Store
5050 West Way
Miami, Florida 00000

Dear Mr. Ball,

In response to your advertisement posted in the front window for a cashier's position, I have enclosed my résumé for your review.

My qualifications for the position include the completion of a two-year business course requirement at Miami Dade High School in Miami, Florida. I completed the course work with a GPA of 3.8 and currently hold the highest award title, Business Student of the Year. I am skilled in sales, customer service, and accounting.

I look forward to meeting with you to discuss my qualifications and the opportunity to know your company in detail.

I will call on Monday, January 10, 2013, to schedule a convenient time to meet with you. Thank you for your time.

Sincerely,

David Crockett

Preparing a Reference Sheet

A reference sheet is needed for the employer to both verify background and employment information and get an objective view of your character and work traits.

First: Identify at least six people who would speak positively about your character, work values, and ethics. Three of the six individuals should know you very well. They should be familiar with your long- and short-term career goals, knowledgeable of your educational aspirations, and aware of the progress you have made toward your goals. You will be using them as your personal references, so choose wisely. The other three individuals should be able to speak intelligently about your professional self. They should be aware of your career and educational experiences. They should be able to speak of your accomplishments and contributions in the work world, your experience as a volunteer or a member of relevant organizations, and your educational success.

Your references could include a trusted teacher, coach, clergy, or school administrator. Also, consider asking an employer who hired you through a vocational program, and certainly any organizations for which you volunteered.

Select anyone with a good reputation you know and trust who could be a reference for you.

Second: Ask each individual for permission to be used as a reference. Then ask those who approve your request if they feel they can give you a positive reference.

Third: Give them a copy of your résumé for their review and comments.

Fourth: Ask each of your references to review your résumé and encourage them to ask questions if they have any. You want to satisfy their curiosity so they can speak with total confidence if questioned by your prospective employer.

Fifth: Inform them of the positions you're applying for; this prepares them if questioned by the employer.

Sixth: Show your appreciation by sending a thank-you note for their support. No matter how close a person is to you, a small gesture showing gratitude puts a smile on their face and a warm place in their heart for *you*.

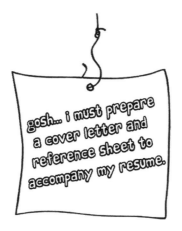

Sample Reference Sheet

Name: **Sophia Johnson**   Position: Cashier

REFERENCE SHEET

PROFESSIONAL REFERENCES

Ms. Mary Carter
1814 Lovelane, Peaceful, Ohio 12345
(000) 000.0000
Job Title: Department Manager

Ms. Cindy Kent
360 Happiness Peak, Peaceful, Ohio 67890
(000) 000.0000
Job Title: Sales Supervisor

Mr. Morris Cabbell
2722 Goodwill Ave., Peaceful, Ohio 01293
(000) 000.0000
Job Title: Accounting Unit Supervisor

PERSONAL REFERENCES

Ms. Nancy Smith
3704 Adventure Rd., Peaceful, Ohio 34567
(000) 000.0000

Mr. James Richburg
732 Rhythm Rd., Peaceful, Ohio 67890
(000) 000.0000

Mr. Randy Gonzales
1453 E. 92nd St., Peaceful, Ohio 12345
(000) 000.0000

A teen with a résumé illuminates confidence and professionalism.

CHAPTER 5

Interviewing

113

Sophia

Do you recall in Chapter 1 that Sophia was unsure about the career path required to become a pharmacist?

Well, persistence and hard work paid off. She took a self-assessment, explored the results, and researched the companies that offered opportunities to work in the health care industry—as close to pharmaceutical work as possible. She took the information learned about self, the job, and potential employers, and then prepared a tailored résumé. It landed her an interview with a major hospital as an intern in its research lab.

Sophia was well prepared for the interview. She identified possible interview questions and prepared answers to them. She put the questions and their answers on index cards, then had her friend help her practice out the best responses loud.

Yep! Sophia got the job. Landing her first job as an intern doing research put her one step closer to becoming a pharmacist.

Overview

The interview with the employer is the most important step of the job search process. Your well-written résumé and cover letter are the tools that get you *to* the interview. It's in the interview that you let your employer know why you should be hired.

This is quite different than the *informational interview* discussed in Chapter 2. There, you interviewed people working at particular jobs to see if you might like their type of work. Now, you're preparing for a specific interview with a possible future employer.

Just what does the word *interview* mean? When you break the word down into its smallest parts, the first part "inter" means *between* and the second part "'view" means to *look at*. Here, the word interview is defined as *communication taking place between two people looking at each other.*

This is what goes on during an interview. Ideally, both the interview*er* and the interview*ee* are exchanging information and actively listening to one another.

Once you get to the interviewing phase of your job search, all of the hard work you put into it is likely to pay off. However, to ensure success at this point, let's discuss the interviewing process, effective strategies, and questions that may be asked during an interview.

Tip: Have someone practice an interview
with you. This will help make you
feel more confident and at ease.

The Interviewing Process

The interviewing process has four major parts. If you can clearly define each part and understand *your role* as well as the *employer's role* in all four parts, you're on your way to landing that important job.

Part One – The Introduction

Your introduction is critical. Employers form their *first impressions* at this stage. People decide about you in a matter of seconds. Therefore, within the first few minutes of an interview, know you're being sized up.

Remember, you only get one chance to make a good first impression. And impressions seldom change during the interview. To guarantee a good start and make a positive first impression, be prepared and look your best. Arrive at least 15 minutes early. Be aware of your body language. Greet everyone you come in contact with politely and with a smile. Show enthusiasm and give a firm handshake.

Part Two – The Employer's Agenda

The employer's goal is first to determine if your skills and abilities match the job and then identify if you would fit into the company. Skills and personality are both important in determining the right fit.

The employer also needs to find out as much as possible about you to make a hiring decision. The interviewer wants to know why you're applying for the job, how your skills and experience can help the company, if you'll fit in with others working there, and how much money your services will cost. Most likely, interviewers won't ask you those questions directly, but they are trained and skilled in asking probing questions.

It's your responsibility to be prepared to answer each question truthfully and with substance. Pay attention to the questions commonly asked later in this chapter.

Most important, remember that employers look for positive, "can-do" candidates who are self-starters and eager to accept a challenge.

Part Three – The Applicant's Agenda

It's always *your* responsibility to tell an employer you are interested in the job, company, and/or career field. Convince that person you're the best-qualified candidate for the job.

Basically, you want the employer to know you provide a solution to problems needing to be solved. Help make the interview a dialogue rather than a one-sided conversation. If you speak with authenticity and enthusiasm, then people will find you interesting.

In your interview, say with sincerity what matters most to you about the job. After all, others will get excited about things *you* get excited about.

It's always important to ask questions to show your interest in the job. Although it's best to limit your questions to four or five, if further clarification is needed, go ahead and ask as many questions as needed. Remember your goal: to determine if *you* want to work for that company and if your skills match the job requirements. You're also finding out if the company can provide growth potential for your future.

Be prepared by planning what questions to ask, placing your most important ones at the top of the list. Make sure all your questions are job related.

Specifically, ask about the challenges of the position and confirm that you *understand the issues* before you share how you can help solve them. Before the interview ends, ask the interviewer about any questions or areas he/she would like you to elaborate on. One exception: *Do not ask questions about salary or benefits until a job offer has been made.* Keep in mind you're there to determine if a fix exists. You always have the right to decline an offer if the money isn't right for you.

Part Four – The Closing

At the end of your interview, thank the employer for his/her time. Then ask about the next step in the interview process. If a second interview is required, find out who will interview you and when you can expect a call. Or, if a second interview is not required, ask when a hiring decision will be made.

Get permission to call back if you haven't heard from anyone by a specified date. Close the interview with a firm handshake and a positive, upbeat statement.

Ask for a business card with the employer's name, telephone number, e-mail, and business address so you can send a thank-you note. Handwrite it on quality paper and recap the main points of the interview. Keep it to half a page.

In your note, reflect the same positive attitude and enthusiasm shown at the interview. Etiquette experts say an e-mail thank you is appropriate if previous communications have been conducted using e-mail. Since hiring decisions are made quickly, an e-mail thank you instantly keeps your name in front of the interviewer. Therefore, you may also send your thank you note by e-mail.

Interviewing Strategies

What is your goal during the interview? *To find out as much as you can about the job, while presenting yourself as positively as possible.*

Because good performance in the interview is essential to landing the job, learn how to keep the interview moving in the direction you want it to go. Candidates have the most success when they know themselves, know what they want, and know how to relate it to the employer.

During the interview, potential employers are likely curious to know if your interests, skills, values, salary requirements, and desired level of responsibility match what they have to offer. Either directly or indirectly, employers will ask (1) *Why are you here?* and (2) *What can you do for me?* Be prepared to answer these questions for yourself.

Research

Research the company where you're interviewing to make a good impression and become knowledgeable about your potential workplace. Employers want to meet candidates who have taken the time to learn about their company. As a result, you're demonstrating to the interviewer you have a plan and are thorough.

Doing extensive research will help you develop questions about the industry, company, job, and employer to ask during the interview. It will allow your conversation during the interview to go smoother. The more you learn about the company, the more you have in common with the interviewer.

Have you noticed? One of the quickest ways you can relate to another person is by finding something of common interest to talk about. As you do this, be authentic—all while mastering the art of relating to anyone of any age, gender, culture, or background.

You'll find that doing research will increase your confidence level, and you'll be able to make a more informed decision about the company. Clearly, your decision to work for a company should be based on your awareness of its strong and weak points.

Although research alone won't land you the job, it will give you an advantage over other candidates. It clearly separates an organized applicant from those who are not prepared. It also ensures you're not wasting your time pursuing companies you have no interest in.

Written Materials

Review each company's written materials. Most employers try their best to represent themselves in print. Corporations, public and private agencies, and small businesses produce annual reports and newsletters about their operations. They're eager to provide this information to you because they regard such distribution as good relations with the public. You can also locate this information online in addition to finding names and addresses of companies from publications in your local library.

Networking

Networking with people is one of the most important things you can do in your job search.

Developing a network of people who can provide you with valuable information about prospective employers, opportunities, fresh leads, and encouragement will keep you a step ahead of your competition.

Begin your networking by talking with teachers, friends, relatives, neighbors, and community leaders and letting them know that you are looking for employment. Share important opinions with them such as the type of employment you're interested in, the distance you're willing to travel, and when you are available.

Social Media

Facebook, Twitter, MySpace, LinkedIn, instant messages, and blogs can complement your job search if used properly. Using these sites can boost your network, increase your exposure, provide helpful information, and help you make valuable connections.

However, there is a growing concern about how employers use social media. For the most part, they look to social media to conduct background checks on applicants because social media sites can contain a wealth of information.

Employers are able to access information about you that you didn't intend, such as your age, marital status, political affiliations, personal associates, and attitudes on the many topics you share on your sites. Some employers search sites on potential candidates to identify inappropriate behaviors that might negatively affect the company. In either case, the information gained may be applied when deciding to hire you—or *not* hire you.

Always be careful. Use good judgment about what you share on these sites as it can negatively affect you without your knowing it. Also be aware of potential dangers, such as identity theft, sexual predators, stalking, and unintentional fame and defaming of character. Let's discuss each of these.

Identity theft: Do not share personally identifiable information (PII) such as your date of birth, social security number, place of birth, or information that can be used to uniquely identify you. Until you are 100 percent sure those you communicate with are truly who they say they are, don't share information you do not want the public to know. Conduct your own investigation to make sure the person you are communicating with is authentic. If you receive an e-mail from a potential employer requesting PII information, verify that person's identity before releasing anything.

Sexual predators: These dangerous people are attracted to social media sites because it's easy for them to hide behind false identities. Many sites contain a wealth of personal information they could use inappropriately to misguide you. Follow your intuition and get the proper authorities involved if necessary.

Stalking: It can be easy for people to access and read your private e-mails and messages. Some social media sites allow individuals to know your precise location at specific times. Always take precaution and understand how social media's privacy settings apply to you.

Unintentional Fame or Defaming Character: Photos and video posting can be shared easily, so be cautious about posting certain images, video, or social media clips. You don't want to be caught off guard in an embarrassing situation. Before posting anything, ask, "Do I want my parents or new boss to see this?" As you know, people can alter photos with computer software, so be especially cautious about putting images on the internet.

Caution: Just know that when you post anything on a social media site, it's available to the world. So make sure you never post anything that could put you in harm's way. Read and understand the site privacy clauses and ask questions if you are not sure what they mean. Know that information posted on internet sources is generally considered public. What's posted on web page profiles are generally considered voluntary disclosures. Employers are not generally restricted from accessing this information.

Think carefully before you post. Always question if this item could prevent you from getting an interview or a job—now or in the future!

"Acing" the Interview

Knowing exactly what you want and don't want to say during the interview will help you make a good impression. Well ahead of time, think about what you want to say and write it down. Memorize your skills that are relevant to the job.

Think of an interview as a two-way communication exchange between an interviewer and interviewee. It involves both verbal and nonverbal communication. So focus both on the content of what you'll say and what your body language or nonverbal messages express. To conduct a successful interview, the interviewee must understand the significance behind each question asked. The following addresses what the interviewer is *really* trying to ask without being direct. It also shows how intangible assets are identified and valued in the decision-making process.

There are four basic areas the interviewer focuses on to determine if you are a match for the position and the company.

First: The *professional* you: Will you be loyal, reliable, and trustworthy? This will reveal to the employer the degree of respect you'll have both for your job and the company.

Second: Your *skills*: Will they meet the requirements of the job? Can you do the job and the level of training required to be productive and successful?

Third: Your *achievements/accomplishments*: Do you have past achievements that show a good prediction of your future performance? This can be best demonstrated by using examples that explain the impact of your actions and their outcomes.

Fourth: The *personal* you: What type of person are you? How do you feel about yourself and your chosen career or ideal career? What would you be like to work with? Would you be a team player? Your answers to the employer's questions should be positive, not negative, and should emphasize your strengths, not weaknesses.

Remember, the interviewer also wants to know what your weaknesses are. When answering your questions, make sure you keep both the substance and the form of your answers positive. For example, words such as *couldn't, can't, won't,* and *don't* can create a negative tone and detract from the positive and enthusiastic image you want to display.

During the interview, be sure to provide brief, to-the-point answers that relate your skills and experience to the needs of the employer. When possible, include what you know about the company obtained through research and networking in your answers.

Interview Questions

As stated earlier, practice for the interview by anticipating what questions might be asked and prepare your answers ahead of time.

Preparation and *practice* is the key to doing your best. Most of the questions will relate to educational background, relevant experience, career goals, personality, and related concerns. Review the frequently asked questions that follow, prepare your answers to them, and practice those answers out loud. Have a friend or family member practice with you to help you perfect this skill. Be sure to rehearse with someone who will give you constructive criticism as well as positive feedback.

Notes to myself...
1. Review research notes.
2. Prepare anticipated interview questions and answers.
3. Ask a trusted source to listen to me practice out loud.
4. Write the questions and answers on index cards.

Frequently Asked Questions

Education

- Describe your educational background.
- What is your major field of study?
- Why did you choose this field?
- What subjects did you enjoy the most? Why?
- What subjects did you enjoy the least? Why?
- Tell me about the best/worst teacher you ever had.
- What is your grade-point average? Describe your learning style.
- What leadership positions have you held?
- Why were your grades so low? How were you able to maintain such high grades?
- What are your plans for furthering your education?
- What new skills do you hope to gain through education?
- If you could start your educational journey all over, what would you do differently?
- Where do you want to be five years from now?

Work Experience (Paid and Unpaid)

- What other jobs have you held?
- What were your major achievements in past jobs?
- What is your typical workday like?
- What skills do you enjoy using the most?
- What did you like about the workplace?
- What did you dislike?
- Which job did you enjoy most? Why?
- Which job did you least enjoy? Why?
- Tell me about a problem you solved.
- How do you handle difficult people?
- What tools do you use to resolve conflict?

Career Goals

- Why did you leave your last job?
- Why do you want to work for our company?
- Why do you think you are qualified for this position?
- Why are you looking for another job?
- Ideally, what would you like to do?
- Why should we hire you?
- How would you improve our operations?
- What do you want to be doing five years from now?
- What do you want to be earning five years from now?
- What are your short-term goals? (One-year time frame)
- What are your long-term goals? (Two to five years)
- When will you be ready to begin work?
- What attracted you to our organization?
- How do you feel about working overtime?

Personality and Other Concerns

- Tell me about yourself.
- What are your major weaknesses?
- What are your major strengths?
- What causes you to lose your temper?
- Do you have any hobbies?
- What do you do in your spare time?
- What type of books do you read?
- What role does your family play in your career?
- How well do you work under pressure?
- When you have a deadline, how do you handle it?
- Are you a self-starter?
- What type of traits do you prefer in people you work with?
- How creative are you?
- If you could change your life, what would you do differently?

Next, let's examine questions that employers should *not* ask during an interview. Understanding these forbidden questions will better prepare you to interview well.

Forbidden Interview Questions

Are there illegal questions an employer should not ask you? Yes, normally these types of questions pertain to age, citizenship, disability, equal pay/compensation and sex discrimination, genetic, national origin, pregnancy, race/color, religion, sex, sexual harassment, ancestry, credit rating, criminal record, military discharge, and religion.

Although the intent of these questions may be to determine if you are a good fit for the job, it's important to know that *only information relevant to your ability to do the job* can and should be asked.

Employers may not be aware of the law and ask a forbidden question. This can turn a good interview into a bad one if you don't know the law or how to respond. Be sure you have a basic understanding of regulations that govern job discrimination.

Now and as you advance through your career journey, become familiar with Discrimination Laws and Federal Equal Employment Opportunity (EEO) Laws by visiting: www.eeoc .gov/facts/qanda.html

Review these sample forbidden questions to increase your awareness.

Examples of Forbidden Questions
Nationality
  ◆ Incorrect: Are you a United States Citizen?
    The employer wants to know you are legally able to work for the company.

- Correct: Are you authorized to work in the United States?

Religion

- Incorrect: What religion do you practice?
  The employer wants to know if you're available to work the weekend schedule.
- Correct: What days are you available to work?

Age

- Incorrect: How old are you?
  The employer may ask questions about your age to determine your maturity level, if you're old enough to work, or if you're close to retirement.
- Correct: Are you older than 18 years of age?

Marital and Family Status

- Incorrect: Is this your maiden name?
  The employer may be interested in your marital status.
- Correct: Have you worked or earned a degree under another name?
- Incorrect: Do you have or plan to have children?
  The employer is trying to determine if family obligations will get in the way of work hours.
- Correct: Are you available to work overtime on occasions? Can you travel?

Gender

- Incorrect: How do you feel about male/female supervisors?
  The employer may want to know how well you work with people of the opposite and/or same sex.
- Correct: Tell me about your experience managing teams?

Wow... The EEOC website has a lot of information on laws, regulations, and guidance that prohibit discrimination.

I must remember to visit their site at www.eeoc.gov!

Discrimination Laws and Federal Equal Employment Opportunity (EEO) Laws

Age Discrimination in Employment Act: Involves treating someone (an applicant or employee) less favorably because of age; protects individuals who are 40 years of age or older

Disability Discrimination: Involves unfavorably treating a qualified individual with a disability due to a disability

Equal Pay/Compensation and Sex Discrimination: Makes it illegal to discriminate based on sex in pay and benefits

Genetic Information Discrimination: Makes it illegal to discriminate against applicants and employees because of genetic information

National Origin Discrimination: Involves unfavorably treating people (applicants and employees) because they come from a particular country or part of the world, or because of ethnicity or accent, or because they appear to be from a certain ethnic background

Pregnancy Discrimination: Involves unfavorably treating a woman because of pregnancy, childbirth, or a medical condition related to pregnancy or childbirth.

Race/Color Discrimination: Race discrimination involves unfavorably treating someone (applicants or employees) because he/she is of certain race or because of personal characteristics associated with race, such as hair texture, skin color, or facial features. Color discrimination involves treating someone unfavorably because of skin color or complexion.

Religion: Involves unfavorably treating a person (an applicant or employee) because of his or her religious beliefs or because that person is married to (or associated with) an individual of a particular religion or because of his/her connection with a religious organization or group

Sex: Involves unfavorably treating someone (an applicant or employee) because of the person's gender or sexual orientation

Sexual Harassment: It is unlawful to harass a person (an applicant or employee) because of that person's sex. Harassment can include "sexual harassment" or unwelcome sexual advances, requests for sexual favors, and other verbal or physical harassment of a sexual nature.

Immigration Reform and Control: Involves asking questions about citizenship before making a job offer

Caution: If you're asked an illegal question during an interview, politely avoid answering it by saying, "Wow, I've never been asked that before" and then chuckle. This will give the employer the opportunity to redirect the conversation.

You may have to refuse to answer a question. If so, simply do so tactfully. If the employer persists with illegal questions, you have the right to terminate the interview.

Keep in mind you're there to gain information about the employer so you can decide if it's a good fit for *you*. Improper questions could be a sign that it's not a good place for you to work. You can politely excuse yourself and thank the interviewer for his or her time.

Behavior Interview Questions

As you advance through your career journey, the interviewer's questions may become more complex. He or she may ask behavior-type questions to learn how you react in given situations. They're designed to let you talk about your previous experiences in a way that gives the interviewer insight into how you behave in certain situations. The interviewer develops these questions to match the job composition and determine if you're a good fit for the job.

Again, this is why conducting research on the job, company, and organizational culture is important. In this case, you want to be prepared to provide examples of your work-self. You also want to explain situations, identify your role, share outcomes, and demonstrate how you made a positive difference. To do so, carefully listen to the interviewer's questions so you can describe in detail your response.

Here's an example of a behavioral interview question:

Interviewer: "Can you give me an example of a problem you faced on the job or in school, and tell me how you solved it?"

The Strategy: This question tests your critical thinking skills and tells the interviewer how you solve problems. Ideally, the problem you use as an example should be similar to the type of problem you're likely to face at the job you're interviewing for.

Remember, prepare your answers ahead of time. Put each question on an index card and have a friend or family member ask you the questions. This will give you the opportunity to practice out loud. Then practice, practice, and practice some more until your responses flow naturally.

I must remember to answer behavior
interview questions by:

1) Describing a problem and how I dealt
   with it, AND

2) Using examples that are relevant
   to the job I'm interviewing for.

General Tips and Guidelines

Keep these tips in mind when preparing for an interview:

✓ Think before you speak.

✓ Respond intelligently to all questions.

✓ Effectively communicate your personal and professional traits. Balance yourself; sell your skills, detail your experience and abilities, show your dynamic personality; maintain a positive attitude.

✓ Do *not* talk about salary or fees unless the employer brings up the issue first. If unsure of the starting salary, ask what the company will pay an individual with your skills and experience. Do not short yourself by agreeing to or requesting a salary before doing your research. Your ultimate goal? Not to mention salary until an offer has been made.

✓ At this stage in your career journey, time is important. Make sure the employer can accommodate your hours of availability.

Preparing Thank-you Letters

✓ Format your thank-you letter as a business letter.

✓ Address your thank-you letter to the person who interviewed you.

✓ Make certain you have the correct spelling of the interviewer's name; include the title, organization, and complete mailing address.

✓ Express your appreciation for hosting the interview, touring the facilities, and meeting many of the employees.

✓ Re-emphasize your skills and qualifications that match the job; address how the company can gain from them.

✓ Briefly include information of importance you forgot to mention during your interview.

Body of Your Thank-you Letter

1. **Paragraph One:** Express appreciation for the interviewer's time. Mention things you were appreciative of such as the tour of the facilities, meeting the employees, getting an overview of the company's purpose and future goals.

2. **Paragraph Two**: Re-emphasize your desire to work for the company. Tell how your skills perfectly match the job. Talk about the contributions you could make to the company in that position.

3. **Paragraph Three:** Close with a sincere thank you and state that you will follow up.

A sample of a thank-you letter follows.

Sample Thank-you Letter

January 10, 2013

Ms. Maria Mead, Supervisor
Lucky Food Super Center
00000 Laurel Way
San Francisco, California 00000

Dear Ms. Mead,

I appreciated the interview opportunity at Lucky Food Super Center on Monday. The tour of the store and your overview of the store's setup and function gave me a clear understanding of the cashier's position. In particular, I was impressed with the state-of-the-art point of sales terminals and the quality of customer service you expect to be rendered.

The entire experience has confirmed my desire for employment as a cashier with Lucky Food. My completion of a two-year business course has prepared me well for this position. Based on my interview, I know I am a perfect candidate for the job and will fit in well with the Lucky staff.

Thank you for the experience of getting to know your organization better. I look forward to hearing from you in the near future. I will contact you within a week to obtain the status of the hiring process.

Sincerely,

Sumsing Wong
001 Aladdin Way
San Francisco, California 90001
Telephone Number: 000-100-0000
E-mail Address: name@e-mailaddress.com

*Actively listen and ask questions.
It is up to you to determine
the fit between your skills and
the company's requirements.
This will help you make good
career decisions about
each job you research.*

CHAPTER 6

The Employer's Perspective

Overview

"Would I hire me?" It may sounds silly to ask that question, but this is a time to do an honest self-examination. Employers will want to know if they hire you, "what's in it for me?" That's a fair question and one you can become more prepared to answer as you go through this chapter.

The preceding chapters described how to conduct a successful job search. You were introduced to **self-assessment tools** to identify your likes and dislikes; you learned how to **research** the company to gather helpful and insightful information; then you practiced completing an **employment application.** You were exposed to the basic formats of **résumé** writing, and taught how to conduct *win-win* **interviews**.

Now it's time to put all of these together! So, let's review the **employer's perspective** and fine tune the information you have studied. You're now ready to apply this knowledge in the real world.

The "employer's perspective" that follows is compiled of responses to a survey that 100 employers kindly completed and returned. The employers surveyed come from a range of businesses and a variety of career fields.

Respondents were required to meet these criteria:

- ◆ Experienced in interviewing individuals aged 15 through 25
- ◆ Had the authority to hire and fire individuals
- ◆ Employed in a company or industry in which the workforce was predominantly between the ages of 15 and 25 years

◆ Demonstrated a strong desire to work with young people and were interested in their success

We asked them to tell us in detail what they *liked* and *disliked* about working with this age group. Then we carefully analyzed and grouped this information into the following three categories:

◆ **The *do* lists.** What employers particularly value in the workplace and therefore what potential employees should attempt to *do* on their applications and during the interview.

◆ **The *don't* lists.** What employers said potential employees should *not do* (*never do*) on their application, during an interview, or after being hired.

Note: The dos and don'ts are listed by category but in no order of *importance.* The caring employers and this author believe that each listed **do** and **don't** is of *equal importance* for you to pay close attention.

Words of wisdom and encouraging messages. The participating employers jotted down tips to support your success in candid ways to assist a young person entering the workforce for the first time.

Application and Résumé *Do* List:

Do...

1. ... be properly dressed when picking up an employment application or delivering a finished application.
2. ... have your résumé and reference sheets available.
3. ... write neatly or type your employment application.

4. ... fill in every line on the application, or at least acknowledge that you have read it by writing "N/A" (non-applicable) in the block.
5. ... list your achievements and awards as they apply to the job or career field.
6. ... list all of your training experiences (i.e., certificates, such as Red Cross certification and/or other community certifications.
7. ... write a detailed description of your past work experiences using examples.

The Interview *Do* List:

1. ... be punctual; however, it's good practice to arrive at least 15 minutes before your scheduled appointment. This shows your eagerness and interest.
    Note: If an emergency comes up, be considerate and responsible enough to call and explain the situation, then reschedule as soon as possible.
2. ... act maturely.
3. ... be particularly neat and appropriately dressed for your interview.
4. ... show good manners; stand up when you are approached by your potential employer and give a firm handshake; always be respectful.
5. ... know and use the employer's name correctly.
6. ... introduce yourself, if necessary.
7. ... be polite, speak clearly, and have direct eye contact with everyone you speak to.
8. ...be cheerful and show high energy; be extremely outgoing to people.
9. ... have a positive attitude and be prepared to sell yourself as a future employee.

10. ... show confidence, be relaxed, and tell people what you are looking for.
11. ... use your people skills well.
12. ... be flexible and open.
13. ... show a willingness to learn.
14. ... research the company and know what they do. (See Chapter 2.)
15. ... be current on industry trends and changes.
16. ... bring your youthful energy and exuberance to the company.
17. ... show plans to stay with the company for a long time.
18. ... state why you are the best person qualified for the job when asked or given a suitable opening. Take the opportunity to plainly state you want the job and will serve the company well.

The Application Don't List

These may prevent you from being hired.

Don't...

1. ... call a company and casually ask if it is hiring.
2. ... yell at people in or outside of their place of business.
3. ... use slang or vulgar language. *It is not acceptable in any business environment.*
4. ... have inaccurate information on your form.
5. ... hand in a torn or stained application.
6. ... use a pencil to fill in an application.
7. ... turn in a sloppily written application.
8. ... use white-out or make scratch outs.
9. ... make repetitive statements on your application or résumé.
10. ... hand in an incomplete application.

11. ... turn in an unsigned form.

The Interview Don't List

Don't...

1. ... be tardy; if you're not on time for the interview, employers will rightly assume you most likely won't show up for work on time.
2. ... bring friends to the interview; *never* say you must leave because someone is waiting for you.
3. ... have poor hygiene, e.g., be unshaven or have bad breath, body odor, long unkempt hair, or poor grooming habits (dirty nails, bitten nails, chewing on your hair, etc.).
4. ... chew gum or have candy in your mouth.
5. ... dress trendy or "street-like" (i.e., shorts, tank tops, flip flops, etc.). It shows a lack of professionalism and inconsideration for the potential employer.
6. ...show excessive nervousness; yet, on the flip side, try not to be too reserved either.
7. ...have poor body language (e.g., slouching, sitting on the edge of the chair, being stiff and unapproachable like you have a chip on your shoulder).
8. ...cross your arms; this body language is known to show a negative attitude.
9. ...give simple *yes* or *no* answers during an interview, causing the employer to do all the talking.
10. ...mumble your answers; employers want you to be direct, clear spoken, and articulate.
11. ...use slang phrases such as "you know" or "like"; this is immature and disrespectful.
12. ...give long answers to questions or be a "know it all."
13. ...be irresponsible, careless, or unfocused.
14. ...repeat yourself.

15. ...use expressions such as "um," which could mean you're easily distracted, unsure of yourself, or impolite.
16. ...leave your answers unfinished.
17. ...jump to conclusions before a question or statement is completely voiced.
18. ...interrupt during a conversation.
19. ...elaborate on your negative qualities.
20. ...show a lack of experience. They expect you to be ambitious and motivated, so you might share volunteer experiences or information about providing assistance to your neighbors or community.
21. ...complain about previous employers.
22. ...give a negative impression or speak poorly of your personal outlook on life.
23. ...hesitate to speak up and ask questions; it shows an indifference to the job and company, which means *the job is not your priority.*
24. ...look at the floor, ceiling, or elsewhere; keep your eyes on the person interviewing you. *Be careful to not give the impression that you are an indifferent, uncaring person.*
25. ...stare into space; it implies you're not interested nor mature enough for the job.
26. ...state that you aren't impressed by the employer's company.
27. ...request time off before you start working.

After-You-Are-Hired Don't List

Don't...

1. ...have excessive absences. The company rightfully expects you to be there on time as scheduled.
2. ...miss your work commitments and deadlines set by the company.

3. ...stand around idle; use this time to be creative and find work to keep busy.
4. ...complain, gossip or associate with those who like to spread rumors
5. ...be playful and not pay close attention to instructions.
6. ...use the work phone or your cell phone excessively, or use your cell phone while assisting customers.
7. ...have long and/or frequent visits with your friends.
8. ...be late returning from breaks or lunch.
9. ...complain about others and your supervisor to co-workers.
10. ...take personnel matters to a higher-level manager before first going to your supervisor.
11. ...show a negative attitude about taking on extra duties.

Words of Wisdom and Encouraging Messages

Employers passed on the following **words of wisdom** and **encouraging messages** to teens looking for a job. We used each employer's exact wording so you'll understand the true importance of their expectations.

- "Dress for success when picking up and dropping off employment applications."
- "Anything excessive is unattractive."
- "If not hired by one employer, do not take it personally; keep going for what you want and what will make you happy."
- "Be serious about whatever you are out to achieve."
- "Stay focused, friendly, and reliable."
- "When searching for a job, always be prepared with transportation to make it to the interview.
- "Always remember to look and feel your best!" (*This is an attitude, and it's within your control.*)
- "Be yourself and let your personality shine through."

- "Take classes to prepare for the job search process."
- "Relax, think positive, and be confident."
- "Have a positive attitude and be confident."
- "Do the best you can do at each job. Any previous job performances will affect future job opportunities. Don't be discouraged."
- "Work hard! You'll move up in life."
- "During the interview, sell yourself to the company."
- "Eye contact is the key."
- "Be persistent if you want to go after the job, and always follow up."
- "Appearance and attitude are very important."
- "Be polite, smile a lot, and make yourself available to work. The more wide open your availability, the more attractive you become."
- "Be mature, don't be shy, and *do* look professional."
- "Be persistent when looking for work. Be friendly and outgoing; make good eye contact. You'll often get put off or discouraged in your job search, but don't take it personally. Most companies interview a lot of applicants just for *one* position."
- "Sell yourself to the interviewer."
- "Be positive, be professional, relax, do the best job, give 100 percent not 90 percent. Be aggressive and always remember to smile!"
- "Educate yourself on the position you're applying for. Always make eye contact, speak clearly, and don't give one-word answers. Back up your answers."
- "If you're going to work for others, be sure to give them your *all* and be prepared to learn. Remember that someday you will be in their position helping another young person."
- "If you put in 110 percent all the time, you can be confident you've tried your best."

Job Search Skills

Employers were also requested to comment on three areas *critical* to the success of a job seeker: **communication skills, transferable skills, and body language**.

The following tips will contribute to having a positive experience while conducting a successful job search and being employed.

Communication Skills

1. Be an effective listener and pay attention.
2. Speak clearly and use examples or tell about the actual event when explaining your work experience.
3. Give direct answers and explain your actions.
4. Don't take your parents with you to look for a job and have them do the talking for you.
5. Be articulate; clearly communicate your ideas.
6. Be flexible.
7. Be attentive to the person you are talking with.
8. Pronounce words properly. You do not talk to adults the same way you talk to your friends. That means *no slang!*
9. Speak to everyone with respect and listen to what people have to say.
10. Learn how to resolve conflicts and relate to others.
11. Be prepared to ask questions.
12. Be honest and polite.
13. Be well spoken and talkative; do not use slang.
14. Be conscious of using good posture.
15. Turn the power off on all electronic devices. If you wish to use your tablet, laptop, or smart phone to take notes, request permission first.

Transferable Skills

1. Playing sports teaches teamwork.
2. Babysitting jobs and paper routes give a sense of responsibility.
3. Prior work experiences teach universal skills.
4. Be able to listen, give advice, and share with others—all great people skills.
5. Tracking and record keeping shows you've been responsible for your daily course schedules and staying on top of assignments.
6. Meeting deadlines and turning in class assignments on time prepares you well for work.
7. Public relations: Holding an elected position in school or joining a respected club prepares you to know how to speak with people and handle workplace relations.
8. Pleasant personality and good attitude go a long way.
9. Computer lab experience provides technical skills.
10. Salesmanship: Speaking and presenting ideas to your school's student body shows you're better prepared for the sales workforce.
11. Outgoing, enthusiastic, and friendly personality are strong selling points. Everything else can be taught; these traits can't.
12. The ability to work well with others is required.
13. Leadership: Showing initiative—such as taking the lead in extracurricular activities—will serve you well in the work world.

Body Language

1. Sit up straight. Don't squirm around in your seat.
2. Make good eye contact and try not to make nervous fidgeting movements.
3. Reach out confidently and give a firm handshake.
4. Appear relaxed and at ease while talking with people you don't know.
5. Smile and keep a pleasant look on your face. Nod and show signs of agreement when appropriate. Also show signs of needing more clarity.
6. Avoid the excessive use of your hands when talking.
7. Sit so you look directly at the interviewer.
8. Do *not* cross your arms or have wandering eyes when being interviewed in a busy area.
9. Avoid slouching, biting nails, and sweating.
10. Ladies, pay close attention when crossing your legs. No one wants to see your underwear. Likewise, for men and women, don't show your mid-section and behind by wearing tops that are too short or that rise up in the back.
11. Maintain good posture.

Advice to Keep in Mind

Now that you have carefully reviewed the employer's expectations and compared the information in the preceding chapters, it's time to identify and determine your course of action.

You can start to effectively plan your career path; your job search can be fun and adventurous.

Just remember to be positive and friendly, and always smile. Try not to be nervous about interviewing; after all, it's part of a bigger process.

With all of this information, it's likely your confidence has greatly increased. At this point, the negative stories you've heard about the *job search process* no longer have merit.

From this time forward, you'll no longer talk yourself out of what you have the potential and the will to do. Yes, you're now ready to go out and conquer that job search!

*Be honest and positive.
Remember, knowledge is power
if shared. Act on the employers'
shared words of wisdom.*

CHAPTER 7

Salary Negotiation

WORK VALUES

GOOD ETHCIAL PRACTICES

BE A PROBLEM SOLVER

HAVE A SERVICE MIND-SET

David

David

As a college student, David held several different positions in the criminal justice career field. His personal and work values contributed to getting recognized as a high achiever. Also, his willingness to help others opened up opportunities for him to learn and hone his skills.

David's colleagues viewed him as a team player. He earned various awards and certifications, and he was highly regarded by peers and supervisors.

After college graduation, David applied for his first job and was able to negotiate a higher starting salary than posted based on:

- Previous work experiences
- Certifications earned
- Awards received

He had the proper documentation as proof, including his résumé that reflected the skill-set the employer required.

David's résumé also demonstrated his ability to perform the job and showed career progression. His past performance indicated to the employer his future potential.

As a result, the company's decision-makers knew they were gaining a well-qualified employee.

Overview

As a teenager, at the beginning of your career journey, the types of jobs accessible to you will have non-negotiable salaries and wages. Companies such as retail giants and fast-food employers that depend on a large teen workforce bank on paying teens standard minimum wages. Now, more than ever, it's important that you know your worth, your personal values,

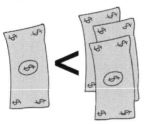

and your work values. The weak economy and changes to minimum wage laws has increased your competition. Today, you're competing with adult job seekers who have solid skills and good work ethics—and are willing to work for low wages.

Knowing what you are worth, while understanding your work and personal values, will increase your confidence and knowledge to negotiate.

Your negotiation can be based on having a highly sought-after skill, specialized training, excellent soft skills, and strong work and personal values. You may also want to negotiate after you have been employed for a time and are performing at a high level that produces noticeable results. For instance, you may be consistently exceeding a company quota. Knowing that provides an opportunity to ask for a salary increase or an item you desire (e.g., training, developmental opportunities, change in work schedule, etc.). Negotiations don't always have to involve money.

To aid your advancement at a fast pace early in your career journey, understand your worth. Also understand the direct correlation between work and personal values and the job's or company's requirements. *This relationship strengthens job security and increases salaries.*

Yes, being clear about what you expect and value in a job can have a direct effect on how much money you can make. That's why it's important to know your values and compare them to the job and the company's culture. If they're compatible, the chances of being successful are greater.

Values include beliefs, attitudes, and judgments. They highlight what's important to you and convey how you feel. More often than not, career choices are based more on personal values than the work itself. That's why it's important to *define* your work values.

Work Values

Work values are attributes that give you job satisfaction. Ideally, these values provide inner satisfaction and motivation, and they lead you to feel and say, "I love my job."

Good work and personal values make up the foundation for good employees. You define *your* work values by asking and answering questions such as, "Do I want to work for a small or large company?", "Is it more appealing working with people or alone?", "Do I like the freedom to carry out my responsibilities independently or with well-defined guidance?"

Work values are the elements you want your work environment to offer. They are the conditions you believe will contribute to your success.

In addition to defining your work values, take time to define your *personal* values. Employers seek employees who demonstrate both work and personal values—characteristics and personality traits that lead to success. To find a good fit between you and a job or career, both kinds of values should be acknowledged with honesty and without judgment.

Personal Values

Personal values are the standards you set for yourself to live by. Since they vary by individual, they can include things such as religion, morals, and ethical practices. In effect, they reflect your internal reference of what is good.

Personal values are the compass for how you interact in your relations. They represent qualities you feel strongly about, such as acceptance, accomplishment, accountability, balance, belonging, dependability, determination, encouragement, enjoyment, financial independence, resourcefulness, thoughtfulness, trustworthiness, understanding, uniqueness, and warm-heartedness.

Know your work and personal values when choosing a job or career. They serve as a gauge for your emotions to measure the degree of happiness and satisfaction you'll experience. How you prioritize your values will change over time. For example, as a teen, you may not consider financial independence important. But as you become an adult with increased responsibilities, your outlook on financial independence will change.

Getting clear about what you expect and *value* in a job can directly affect how much money you can make. So know your skills and values and then compare them to the job requirements and the company's culture. If they're compatible, the chance of being successful increases. Plus, having a strong work ethic and good work values can provide opportunities that may not otherwise be available to you.

A happy employee makes a pleasant and productive one. Enjoying good working conditions is far more important than making an extra dime.

Most important, approach every job with a *service* and *problem solver* mindset. This means you're serving customers with a positive attitude, and you're always looking for ways to improve in the workplace. *Money always comes to those who serve others and fulfill a need.*

Remember, salary negotiations don't always have to be monetary; they can be values-based in the form of career development opportunities, mentoring programs, peer coaching, leadership opportunities, training, and payment for skill-building courses.

Another negotiation opportunity is lateral mobility. Moving to a different position at the same pay rate can enhance your professional and personal growth. Lateral mobility provides the opportunity to gain new knowledge and skills, a chance to expand on accomplishments, and a way to overcome boredom. Ultimately, it can lead to a promotion or bring about potential future opportunities.

If you negotiate for money, make sure you're familiar with your area's salary scales and other conditions for your line of work in addition to the company's promotion policies. This will help you understand any limits and prevent you from taking personally decisions about your pay.

How to Negotiate

If negotiating is part of your hiring strategy, have proof of your specialized skills, training, and experience that warrants a higher wage. If you're negotiating after being hired and consistently performing well, schedule an appointment with your supervisor, then present the facts and results that substantiate your request. It is a good practice to keep a record of your accomplishments and results.

Also during performance reviews, have your own assessment available. If you're not pleased with your performance review, voice your concerns openly with your supervisor.

Lastly, if your work ethic includes any of the items listed under good ethical practices, you will advance at a faster pace than your counterparts who lack good ethical practices. Having solid work and personal values will strengthen your position when requesting an increase in salary ahead of schedule or when you take a lateral move.

Good Ethical Practices

1. Show up for work on time.
2. Strive for perfect attendance.
3. Perform with excellence.
4. Be responsible; carry out all assigned duties and responsibilities.
5. Assertively seek out additional duties and responsibilities.
6. Willingly accept extra work assignments.

7. Provide outstanding customer service.
8. Approach your supervisor directly and ask what you can do to get promoted.
9. Obtain focus and remain focused.
10. Ask for clarification if you don't understand what's expected or what you should be doing.
11. Show interest in your job, expressing that you like what you're doing.
12. Share ideas on how to do the job more efficiently.
13. Foster healthy working relationships.
14. Address your concerns or issues in a positive way.

You'll get promoted faster and be noticed as worthy of a promotion by practicing all of these actions. Getting positive recognition will contribute to your success.

Know What You Value

Know what's important to you in a job. Being clear about what you value most within a job will help you decide if the job is right for you and if you should stay.

Review the following checklists to determine what's most important to you in a job right now. Also keep in mind that your value system will change over time as life circumstances change.

Value Exercise:
Work and Personal Values Important to You

This exercise will help you gain a better understanding of your most significant values.

From this list of values (both work and personal), select the five that are most important to you. They will offer guides for tailoring your job-search communication, a foundation for negotiations, and a satisfying way of life. Feel free to add any values of your own.

Place a checkmark by the items most important to you, then identify your top five values from each of the lists.

Work Values

_____ Working as a team member

_____ Opportunity to learn new things

_____ Helping others

_____ Environment fostering competition

_____ Working environment "inside"

_____ Working environment "outside"

_____ Using your hands

_____ Working with details, data, numbers

_____ Working with *things* and machinery

_____ Working alone

_____ Working with people

_____ Challenging and rewarding work

_____ Good salary

_____ Earning extra income

_____ Performing a variety of tasks

_____ Advancement opportunities on the job

_____ Job recognition

_____ Routine work

_____ Boss's expectations clearly defined

_____ Persuading or influencing others
_____ Flexible work hours
_____ Set work schedule
_____ Freedom of expression
_____ Able to present and implement ideas
_____ Creativity

Personal Values

_____ Ability to work independently
_____ Acceptance
_____ Accountability
_____ Accomplishment
_____ Ambitious
_____ Assertive
_____ Balance
_____ Belonging
_____ Dependability
_____ Determination
_____ Encouragement
_____ Enjoyment
_____ Financial independence
_____ Resourcefulness
_____ Thoughtfulness
_____ Trustworthiness
_____ Understanding
_____ Uniqueness
_____ Warm-heartedness

When you search for a job, keep the items you checked in mind. Look for the job that will offer most of the items deemed important to you. Remember, no one job will have all of those items, so be flexible and open.

Values Employers Look for in Employees

Adaptability	Integrity
Communication skills	Loyalty
Confidence	Motivation
Competence	Positive attitude
Dependability	Professional behavior
Honesty	Responsibility
Interpersonal abilities	Willingness to learn

When negotiating in the workplace, you need to know what you are good at and have the evidence to prove it. Know your worth, work, and personal values as well as the skills you possess that the employer values. This will strengthen your chance of succeeding in your negotiations.

Once you understand the skills and characteristics most employers look for in an employee, you can tailor your job-search communication—the employment application, résumé, cover letter, and your interview language—to showcase how well your background aligns with the employer's requirements.

If you discover you don't hold some of the traits employers' desire of an employee, remind yourself that you're at the *beginning* of your career journey. All of these traits can be learned, developed, and cultivated over time.

The art of salary negotiation will improve as you develop your skills and acquire more experience. It is wise for you to learn negotiation techniques and how to measure your worth to pay at a young age.

In your first few jobs, the pay reflects that you are getting paid to learn and grow in your position—a positive way to look at things. Keep in mind you will eventually get opportunities that have a greater value than money. As mentioned earlier, they include training, mentoring, leadership and other educational opportunities.

*Know your employability skills,
work, and personal values
that employers care about.
Then go after what your heart
dictates, knowing that success
and money will follow.*

CHAPTER 8

"Now That I am Making Money, What Do I Do With It?"

Carlos

Carlos

Carlos is making more money than he ever has in his life. But he's not sure what to do with it. It seems he's spending his money as fast as he earns it.

Carlos decided he wanted to manage his money more wisely. So he started to read books, talk with individuals he viewed as successful, and paid closer attention to how much money he was spending and what he was spending it on. After weeks of being more aware of his behavior, he set out to prepare a money management plan.

During a visit to the credit union, he signed up to take a "Money Smart" class offered there. After completing the class, he created his plan.

First, he identified his wants and needs and then prioritized them. Second, he allocated his money by setting percentages for how he would use it, e.g., 50% saving, 40% spending, and 10% sharing. Third, he reviewed the plan and made changes accordingly.

After sticking to his plan persistent, Carlos was able to purchase a car one year later. He learned it's always best to save for a rainy day!

Overview

Finding a job agreeable to your personality is definitely rewarding. But the ultimate reward is the pleasure you'll feel when the money you earn makes you able to fulfill a financial goal or dream. For this reason, it's important to know how much money you need or want to make *before* you start your job search. This will establish the framework for your job search plan and allow you to narrow your focus on employment opportunities that pay wages close to the financial level you desire.

Before your search, you should have answers to three personal financial questions:

1. How will I use my money?
2. How much money do I need?
3. How often do I need to be paid?

Your answers to these questions will help you determine the amount of money you should make and the number of hours you should commit to an employer so you can achieve your financial goals.

Further, understanding your personal financial needs before accepting a job offer provides you with a sense of satisfaction, thus increasing the chance that you will remain on the job longer. Dissatisfaction with employment is instant when an employee discovers the job will not meet his or her financial obligations. Typically, the employee starts to look for another job. But if you understand upfront how much money you need to meet your financial obligations, look for the opportunities that support your needs. Then you'll stay on the job longer.

Lastly, having a financial plan will also ensure you can continue to enjoy extracurricular school activities. You'll already be aware of the amount of time you'll need to commit to working.

Personal financial decision-making is a vital part of the job search process. As mentioned in Chapter 2, when conducting your job research, formulate questions concerning salary. This is the perfect time because you have nothing to lose or feel uncomfortable about since there is no job offer yet to jeopardize.

Understand that the effort you put into managing your money will reflect the attitude you have developed about money. Personal financial decision-making requires self-knowledge, patience, and consistency if you are to succeed in money-management and accomplishing your financial goals.

Start by creating a money-management plan, which provides a guide for taking control of your finances. This plan will help you set goals, monitor your cash flow, and track expenses.

Realize that having a sound spending and savings plan sets the foundation for long-term financial success. Having a plan ensures you begin using your money wisely right from the time you receive your first paycheck. *You* will be in control of your money instead of letting *your money* controlling you. Plus, you'll be developing healthy spending habits that will serve you your whole life.

Remember, good money-management is supported by a written plan and strict self-discipline. A regular review of your expenses and spending habits will guide your actions and help you achieve your financial goals. Then you'll know where you spend your money, you'll keep it longer, and you won't overspend.

Good Money-management Rules
Know What You Have

The first step to good money-management is to know how much money you have and will have. When calculating your pay, take into consideration standard payroll deductions. These will include federal income tax, state income tax, Federal Insurance Contribution Act (FICA), Medicare, and various local taxes. They may also include mandatory union dues and other items specific to your place of employment

Divide and Conquer

Next, establish percentages on how your money will be used based on your plan. One example might be:

Pay Yourself First – 50% (Savings)

Share – 10% (Tithing or charity)
Spend – 40% (Purchases and expenses)

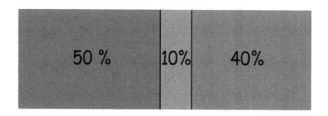

Prioritize Your Plan

To be successful in any planning process, prioritize what's important. You do that by establishing your goal, your savings plan, and your desired outcome.

For example:

Goal: To purchase an Xbox for $250.00 plus tax.

Plan: Save $25.00 each paycheck over 11 biweekly pay periods; this will provide enough money to buy the Xbox and pay the sales taxes.

Outcome: Five months later, you can purchase the Xbox with the $250.00 you've saved.

Review Your Plan and Be Flexible

Reviewing your spending plan helps you prepare for unexpected expenses. Say you're still saving for that Xbox, and you already have $125.00 saved.

During the 11 pay periods in which you are saving, you discover you have to purchase a $25.00 book for your karate class. It's an expense you weren't expecting. In this situation, you can take $25.00 from the Xbox savings and use it to purchase the karate book.

Now is the time to review your spending plan. Instead of the planned five months and two weeks to purchase the Xbox, it will now take six months because you will need the additional paycheck to replace the $25.00 used for karate class.

Be flexible when making adjustments and get back on track!

Financial planning, goal setting, and developing healthy spending habits are indeed challenging but not impossible tasks.

What you think about money and how you value it will influence and form your spending habits. Taking a financial assessment will heighten your awareness of how you feel and think about money. Ultimately, it will help you make better financial decisions.

It will also make you aware of your spending patterns and know what motivates you to spend your money. Self-reflection helps you understand your thoughts and feelings regarding money. Take the assessment at the end of this chapter.

Managing Your Money
Financial Sacrifices

Developing good money-management skills and healthy spending habits requires making sacrifices.

As you've already learned, you first take the time to build a spending plan. When creating the plan, you'll strive to understand the difference between your "needs" and "wants."

Begin your plan by making a list of all your "needs" and their cost. Next, do the same for your "wants." Then compare the totals from each list to your income, which may include your allowance, monetary gifts, payment for work, etc.

If it appears you don't have enough money to buy all of the items on your lists, then prioritize certain ones and make sure you put your primary needs first. Over time, the sacrifices you make will enable you to buy both your "needs" and "wants" while minimizing financial hardship.

Prepare a Spending Plan

A spending plan is a list of items you need or want to buy and their cost. You can create a spending plan for a single activity, such as a recreational Saturday with your friends, or for your yearly school activities.

Regardless of the reason, your goal is to track what you spend so you can get the best bang for your buck.

There are five basic steps in preparing a spending plan:

1. Identify the item(s) you need or want.
2. Determine the cost of each item.
3. Compare the cost to the monies available.
4. Prioritize your needs and wants (and remember that "needs" are more important than "wants.")
5. Establish a spending timeline.

Get in the habit of reviewing your plan regularly to update costs and ensure your actions are leading you in the direction of achieving your goals.

Learning to manage your money at a young age will help you become a better steward over your money as an adult. As you get older and your earnings increase, these skills will put you into a healthier, more rewarding financial lifestyle.

Plan to Save

A spending plan also includes savings. Always pay yourself first, as this is a systematic way to make your money grow. That means whenever you receive money, no matter how much it is, get into the habit of saving a portion. "Paying Yourself First" will become one of your healthiest money-management habits.

Then put your saved money in a financial institution to protect it. You can open a savings account at your local bank or credit union and earn a fee called "interest."

To learn more about savings accounts, visit your local financial institution. The customer service rep can answer your questions and explain different types of savings products available for teenagers.

Self-assessment

Directions: Choose the best answer for each question representing what you do and how you feel and think. Answer only the bonus question that applies to you.

This is not a test (you won't be graded), so answer the questions honestly to increase your self-awareness of how you view and use money.

1. I read money magazines, books, and other materials to learn more about being financially responsible.
   ☐ True   ☐ False

2. I dip into my savings only to buy things I need or things I have already planned to buy and have saved for.
   ☐ True   ☐ False

3. I have identified immediate, short-term, and long-term financial goals.
   ☐ True   ☐ False

4. I habitually save money.
   ☐ True   ☐ False

5. I spend most of my money on things I need and save money to buy things I want.
   ☐ True   ☐ False

6. I make sure the things I buy function in a way that best meet my needs.
   ☐ True   ☐ False

7. I feel bad after making a purchase that I did not plan to buy.
   ☐ True   ☐ False

8. I buy what I need first—before I buy what I want.
   ☐ True   ☐ False

9. I'd rather have money in my pocket than have the most popular thing.
   ☐ True   ☐ False

10. I buy my friends gifts without using my savings.
    ☐ True   ☐ False

Write down your money transactions in a diary, placing each item in one of the following categories: food, clothing, entertainment, recreation, transportation, and "other." Then add the total of each category.

The results indicate how you're spending your money and the amount you have spent. It provides enough information to help you make healthier money-management decisions.

Money-saving Tips

Prepare a spending plan. Keep a balance between what you save and what you spend. Make it a good practice not to spend more than you have. Don't buy what you don't need without planning first. Plan your purchase(s), put them in your spending plan, and buy them when funds are available.

Be creative and explore all options when deciding to make a purchase. Identify ways you can obtain the desired item or service at a reduced cost or no cost at all. This might include coupons or special offers, or buying used items from online auctions, classified ads, yard/garage sales, or people you know.

Swap videos, games, DVDs, and CDs. If you have friends who buy things you like, form a group to swap these items— with your parents' permission, of course. Swapping is a form of recycling, increasing the usage of items without spending any additional money.

Eat at home or pack your lunch. Avoid eating at fast food places and restaurants. Buy food items you can prepare at home and take your lunch to school with you instead of spending money in the cafeteria or vending machines.

To learn more about money, visit these websites:

MoneyInstructor.com

www.moneyinstructor.com

Learn more about basic money skills, personal finance, money-management, business education, career, and life skills.

MyMoney.gov

www.mymoney.gov/content/money-smart-young-adults-financial-education-program.html

Money Smart for Young Adults is a comprehensive financial education curriculum to teach individuals between the ages of 12 and 20 the basics of handling money and finances, including how to create positive relationships with financial institutions.

Teen Money Making Ideas

www.teenmoneymakingideas.com

This educates teens and kids on business, money-management, and money-making ideas in the global economy.

To learn how to get exactly what you need financially to go to college, review this handbook:

Know More No Less Handbook

This is a student/parent handbook you can find online to help you define the annual financial costs of pursuing your post-secondary education interests.

Kid's Money

www.financialplan.about.com

This is an extensive site on teaching kids about money from David McCurrach.

JumpStart.org

www.jumpstart.org

This is a national coalition of organizations dedicated to improving the financial literacy of pre-kindergarten through college-age youth by providing advocacy, research, standards, and educational resources. JumpStart strives to prepare youth for lifelong successful financial decision-making.

The Real Life Money Game

reallifemoneygame.com

The object of the Real-Life Money Game is to let you and your parents collaborate on taking personal responsibility for money your household already spends on your behalf. It provides the opportunity to experience firsthand how money works by giving you control over real money.

CU Succeed Teen Financial Network

www.cusucceed.net/homepage.php?cuid=67358591&PHPSES SID=138988ae9479c6653f6634139dd20a3e

This site contains articles written by teens like yourself. Their topics range from how to manage your money to understanding credit.

It's My Life

pbskids.org/itsmylife

It's My Life features organized topics on money, friends, family, school, body, and emotions. You can read informative articles, share your stories, play games and activities, take quizzes and polls, and watch video clips of other teens talking about their feelings and experiences. Get advice from older teens and experts, and then contribute your own comments and questions.

BECU Financial Service

googolplex.cuna.org/32032/ajsmall/calc.php

This site has a super saving-and-spending calculator you can use to prepare your money-management plan, learn about investing, and learn how to use a lump-sum and periodic-investment calculator.

the more i practice good
spending and saving habits,
the easier it becomes.

$ $ $ $ $

Money Smart Vocabulary

Allowance – An amount of money parents give to their child.

Deposit – Adding money to your savings or bank account.

Goal – Something you are working toward in the future.

Income – Money or earnings a person gets or receives from gifts, allowances, and/or a job.

Interest – The money paid by a bank on the deposits saved in a savings account.

Need – Something you must have or do in order to live.

Saving – Putting your money away in a financial institution for a future goal instead of spending it immediately now.

Spending – Using your money to buy things you want or need.

Want – Something you would like to have but do not necessarily need.

*A wise man knows where
every penny is spent and
dime saved, and is always
prepared for a rainy day.*

CHAPTER 9

If You Must Quit a Job

Chris

Chris found himself in an uncomfortable work situation and realized his job was not a good fit for him. After carefully thinking the situation through and examining discrimination laws, he decided to quit.

Because he understood the importance about not burning bridges, he wrote a letter of resignation and gave a positive reason for resigning. He wanted to leave on a positive note.

By leaving in this manner, he believed the company would give him a good reference. The advantage was he could list this company on future employment applications.

By acting this way, Chris felt confident in his decision the company would do and say the right things in the future to help him advance his career.

Overview

If you discover that a job isn't right for you or perhaps your skills don't suit the workplace and tasks after you've begun working, don't despair. There's a way out.

Not what I expected... HELP!

However, you do not quit a job by failing to show up for work. Instead, take the proper course of action when you want to resign from a job. You have a *moral* and *ethical duty* to follow this course.

First of all, before you consider quitting, try to work things out. Identify the problems you find most unpleasant, and be *specific* in the process to discuss them. Write down your concerns in their order of importance. This will help you keep a better perspective and provide a good reality check for your own peace of mind.

Then once you have determined what the issues are, develop a plan of action. If it's appropriate and the problems aren't directly related to your supervisor, then involve your supervisor; this is part of his or her job. Discuss your concerns openly *and* be receptive to suggestions. Obtain clarification from your supervisor and sincerely attempt to reach a satisfactory solution.

However, if the problem *includes* your supervisor, go to the company's Human Resource representative. Ask the representative to assure you that your name will remain anonymous and the conversation will be kept private. Then discuss your issues and ask for guidance. If it's impossible to work out your problems, *only then* consider the option of quitting. Be wise; there are times when it's better to leave than to stay.

If you decide that quitting is your best alternative, be prepared to follow the proper procedure by resigning both *verbally* and in *writing*. Prepare a resignation letter for the supervisor and for the Human Resources Department. (See a sample resignation letter in this chapter.)

Your written resignation should be brief, to the point, and positive. *Never put your negative thoughts on paper.* The written document will be included in your personnel file and could have a longer lasting effect on your career than the individuals or circumstances you're presently dissatisfied with.

A written resignation reinforces the fact that you're leaving in a way that doesn't pose a threat to the company. Also, it allows you to say what you want to say without interruption or getting sidetracked by unexpected or unsolicited remarks in your oral resignation.

Your oral resignation should be well thought out and presented with courtesy. Carefully choose your words. You do not want to be misunderstood by—nor responsible for burning bridges with—the people you are leaving.

If asked by your current employer or company representative why you're quitting, give a positive answer such as advancing my career. (At this point, whatever you say is going to be viewed as biased.) If the opportunity permits—and only if you feel it is safe to do so—offer suggestions to help the organization operate more effectively.

Do not say or do anything that you may regret later. Keep in mind that even offering constructive criticism can be damaging to your career; therefore, carefully consider your intent and words before speaking.

Do you recall reading about first impressions in Chapter 5? Well, people also remember *last* impressions, and you want their parting perception of you to be favorable and positive. After all, you never know when you might need a reference from someone in that company in the future.

It's polite and, above all, *ethical*, to give the employer at least *two weeks'* notice. Be certain to complete all your unfinished tasks. Don't discuss your circumstances or discontent with co-workers and peers. Continue to be sensitive to others and keep your conversations positive and constructive.

Before departing, spend time nurturing your working relationships; you never know whose path you may cross in the future. Always leave with a positive image.

A sample of a resignation letter follows.

Sample Resignation Letter

January 17, 2013

B. Ball, Owner
My Local Bookstore
5050 West Way
Peaceful, Ohio 56234

Dear Mr. Ball,

I am extremely grateful for the 12 months I have worked for My Local Bookstore. The time employed here has been instrumental to my career and professional development. I sincerely hope that my time with you has likewise contributed to the progress and growth of My Local Bookstore. I am grateful for the opportunity to work with the caliber of professionals at this store, and for the support I have received from upper management.

In order that I may continue in the same professional development, I wish to formally announce my resignation. My last day with My Local Bookstore will be February 1, 2013.

So that the transition is a smooth one, I offer my assistance to those individuals who will inherit my duties and responsibilities.

Sincerely,

Chris Weller
123 Local Street
Peaceful, Ohio 45678
Telephone No.: (000) 100-0001
E-Mail Address: name@e-mailaddress.com

*Never be afraid to leave an
undesirable situation, but
remember to leave gracefully
and ethically. Do not burn the
bridges of your future career.*

CHAPTER 10

Entrepreneurship and You

Candiss

Candiss

Candiss decided to make a career change after working as a telemarketing specialist. She wanted more control over her time as well as use a skill she truly enjoyed—baking deserts. People had always positively commented about her delicious, sweet, and fluffy cupcakes; they frequently requested them for office parties, family functions, and other social gatherings.

So Candiss started her own business selling a selection of specialty cupcakes. To learn more about running a business, she attended the Small Business Administration's (SBA) "Be Your Own Boss" workshop. After completing the workshop, she sought assistance from the SCORE Association. The organization assigned her a mentor to work with her and the rest is history!

Yes, Candiss created her own job! Today, she's an independent, self-employed entrepreneur.

Overview

Entrepreneurship is creating your own job and—even bigger than a job—creating and executing your unique vision. It's an employment strategy that can lead to self-sufficiency and wealth.

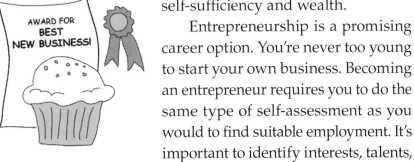

Entrepreneurship is a promising career option. You're never too young to start your own business. Becoming an entrepreneur requires you to do the same type of self-assessment as you would to find suitable employment. It's important to identify interests, talents, and skills you are passionate about that can become profitable. It could be things you do at home in your free time, while you're in school, or when you're with your friends.

Entrepreneurship is starting a business from an idea. It's *creating* a job rather than *accepting* a job. You'll need to be a dreamer and a doer to succeed as an entrepreneur.

Starting your own business can be exciting and rewarding, and it's a lot of hard work. It's serious business.

Before deciding to start your own business, you need to ask and honestly answer this question: "Do I want to alter or give up my extracurricular activities, such as cheerleading, sports, music lessons, dance, and hanging out with family and friends, to run my own business?"

You must be committed and willing to make sacrifices to be successful. There's no simple formula. An entrepreneur identifies something that needs improving, finds ways to do it better, creates a demand for something, or adds value to an existing product. It requires being committed to your ideas and remaining enthusiastic, regardless of what others may say.

Entrepreneurship is unlike working for someone else. It offers the opportunity to use a skill, talent, or interest you enjoy, be your own boss, make your own schedule, experience creative freedom, and gain financial independence. However, entrepreneurship is challenging. In addition to being creative, a hard worker, a leader, and an outstanding planner, it asks you to be a risk-taker to succeed.

Qualities and Traits of Successful Entrepreneurs

Believer – You must believe in your abilities and ideas, even when those who you highly respect do not believe in you or may become discouraging.

Creative – You must have a unique idea or concept that can meet a need, and you must be flexible and innovative to make changes when necessary.

Financially savvy – You must spend money to make money, yet avoid spending more than you make.

Motivated – You must continue to move forward despite setbacks and rejections, holding on to your passion and enthusiasm through all of the negativity.

Persistent – You must be committed to your ideas or concepts and continue moving forward when things come to a standstill.

Positive – You must stay focused. Do not allow yourself to be distracted by negative people or unfavorable events.

Problem-solver – You must keep an open mind and view problems simply as opportunities to make improvements.

Resilient – You must stand strong and work through every issue when challenges and obstacles arise.

Risk-taker – You must be willing to take risks and make risky decisions, and be able to learn how to manage risks while learning from your failures.

Starting Your Own Business

As a young entrepreneur, you can run your own business part time after school or during the weekend.

Starting on a part-time basis allows you to test the waters and build steady revenue. That way, when you're ready to go into business full-time, you'll have existing customers and an income stream.

The information in this chapter is for teens who aspire to become business owners. It's for those ready to take the actions necessary to become self-employed. It requires thinking creatively and differently, stretching your ideas, and expanding your network.

Actions to Take Before Starting a Business

Do your research. Assess the competition and compare your idea with theirs. You want to determine your uniqueness and how you can differentiate your product or service. The information you discover should be incorporated in your business strategy and marketing plan, and used in a manner that gives you the advantage over your competitors. Use the internet to get information on your competitors' product, pricing, service areas, and marketing strategies. You can search by zip code, key words, or company name. Focus on the top 20 businesses.

Ask potential customers, family, friends, and neighbors if they would buy your product or service. Ask what elements are important to them, such as quality, price, functionality, or style. You can also do a test run if appropriate and take the lessons learned to improve on your idea.

Visit your public library to check out resources, such as business journals, magazines, and reference materials, and to use their computers to conduct your research if you do not have a computer.

Choose a business model. A business model is a general description of how a business operates. It shows you how you will generate revenue and profits. When deciding on a business model, be sure to consider how you will reach your customers, promote the uniqueness of your product or service, set your product price, and determine your selling strategy. You'll want to find the right business model for you. Start by examining these business models: (1) online, (2) home-based, and (3) freelance. Then select the model that will work best for your set of circumstances.

The online business model is a relatively low-cost way to start a business. The challenge is directing traffic to your website. You have to invest in search engine optimization, social media practices, and other non-traditional marketing strategies. Since there is very little face-to-face customer contact, it can be challenging to get customers' feedback and build good relations. Teens have been successful starting online businesses selling art, crafts, handmade jewelry, needlecrafts, book markers, and key chains. Other online business ideas are blog writers, web designers, web custom service, and online writers. Learn more by reading the SBA guide *Starting an Online Business.* www.sba.gov/content/starting-online-business.

The home-based business model is another low-risk option. It offers great flexibility and is a low-cost way to start and grow a business. The challenge is maintaining a balance between your business, school, and extracurricular activities. Ideas for home-based business for teens include babysitting, tutoring, writing, painting, dog-walking, tech-related services, house-cleaning service, or neighborhood residential organizer (someone who organizes community yard sales, clean up campaigns, fundraisers, etc.). Learn about starting a home-based business at

www.sba.gov/content/home-based-business.

The freelance business model allows you to be your own boss using a skill or talent you truly enjoy. As a freelancer you contract your services. Most freelancers run their businesses from their homes. They do not own a brick building like a store, or have a professional office like a doctor or lawyer. The benefit of freelancing is it can be done on a part-time basis, giving you time to grow your business and build your customer base. On the other hand, you'll have the challenge of running the business on your own. You are providing the service or product, marketing it, maintaining the finances, and building your network. This can be overwhelming, since you are juggling multiple tasks. Ideas for freelance businesses include writing, graphic design, editing, web design, photography, and computer-related services. To network with other teen freelancers, visit

forum.freelanceswitch.com/topic.php?id=3236.

Whichever business model you choose, consider starting a website to boost your business. The internet has revolutionized business models for most industries and sectors. There are no limits to what you can achieve in this high-tech world.

Select your business type. When you become an entrepreneur, you must decide how you will legally structure your business. The common options are (1) sole proprietorship, (2) corporation, and (3) limited liability company (LLC). Initially, you may not need to select your business type. But as your business grows, you will be required to make a selection. When deciding on your business type, consider how much control you want to have over the business operations and who will receive profits and losses. Understand the liability risks and the tax-rate requirements. It's important to introduce yourself to the different business types to ensure you make an informed decision when the time is right. The following is an explanation of each business type.

A **sole proprietorship** is a business entity that is owned and operated by one individual, and there is no legal distinction between the owner and the business. The owner receives all the profits and has unlimited responsibility for the loss and debts of the business. The business does not exist separately from its owner. Income and losses are taxed on the individual's personal tax return. All you will need is a license and a business checking account to get started. This business type gives you total control.

A corporation is a legal entity that has a separate and distinct legal existence from its owner. Corporations are owned by stockholders or shareholders who share in profits and losses generated through the company's operation. You will need an attorney to assist with setting up a corporation, and you must establish a corporate charter and by-laws. If you set up your business as a corporation, you will have to give some money to the other shareholders in the form of dividends.

A limited liability company (LLC) means that under most circumstances, the owner is not personally liable for the debts and liability of the company. The owner can obtain a tax identification number for the LLC, open a bank account, and do business under its name. If you want complete control, you'll want to set up a single-member LLC. LegalZoom.com provides assistance with setting up LLCs for a fee.

Helpful Resources
Young Entrepreneur
www.gaebler.com/Teaching-Kids-To-Be-Entrepreneurs.htm
This website has many resources for teenagers interested in becoming entrepreneurs.

Entrepreneurship Education
www.entre-ed.org
Visit this website to read teen entrepreneurs' testimonies on how they got started and learn about the education program designed to teach teens about entrepreneurship.

SBA – Small Business Resource

archive.sba.gov/teens/businessbuddy.html

Similar to a buddy list on an instant message site, this site features a compilation of organizations for you to access at the touch of a button. These resources will assist you in counseling, training, and leadership development. Use this list, in addition to other sources on the Internet, to guide you on your path to business ownership.

SBA – Teen's Business Link

archive.sba.gov/teens/

This site contains valuable information on how to start your own business.

Mentor – National Mentoring Partnership

www.mentoring.org

This organization serves young people between the ages of six and 18 by helping find the support and guidance needed to build productive, meaningful lives.

Creative Education Foundation

www.creativeeducationfoundation.org

The purpose of the Creative Education Foundation is to engage and develop the next generation of creative thinkers and innovators.

Teen Entrepreneur

teenentrepreneur.co.za

This site's vision is to cultivate and promote the entrepreneurial spirit in teenagers through seminars, workshops, conferences, and exhibitions.

How to Start a Teen Business from Home
www.ehow.co.uk/how_6113044_start-teen-business-home.html

This site walks you through the steps for starting up your home business.

Books:
The Young Entrepreneur's Guide to Starting and Running a Business – By Steve Mariotti

In this guide, you'll find inspiring stories from young entrepreneurs starting out, as well as stories of successful entrepreneurs such as Mr. Bill Gates, Microsoft cofounder, and Mr. Berry Gordy, Motown founder.

Most important, this guide provides practical steps to entrepreneurship.

Start It Up: The Complete Teen Business Guide to Turning Your Passion into Pay – By Kenrya Rankin

In this book, you'll find comprehensive information on how to identify the best business for you, set up a company, sell your product, and market it. The book also features quotes from successful teen entrepreneurs who turned their dreams into dollars.

The Richest Kids in America: How They Earn It, How They Spend It, How You Can Too – By Mark Victor Hansen

Entrepreneurship Education

Entrepreneurship education is another way for you to learn how to operate a business and discover whether or not business ownership is right for you.

An education program provides information, skills, and motivation to be successful. You learn how to be a better entrepreneur by exploring entrepreneur processes and mentorships. Through these educational programs, you develop leadership and interpersonal skills, improve problem-solving and decision-making abilities, and develop money-management, public speaking, and job readiness skills.

You also learn how to be an effective team player. Many individuals have stated that attending an entrepreneur's education program helped increase their awareness of their career options.

I highly recommend you enroll in a community entrepreneurship education program before starting your own business. For available resources to guide you through the process, visit the United States Small Business Administration's website at

www.sba.gov/content/young-entrepreneurs

Next, I introduce you to amazing young entrepreneurs who are living their dreams and making a big difference doing it. These stories are shared to inspire you, teach you, and show you that opportunities are endless. How did they discover their passion? What were their first steps in building their businesses? Who supported them along the way? Read on!

Stories from Young Entrepreneurs

You are about to read about young entrepreneurs who shared their stories in their own words to inspire you to go after your dream. They disclose information about their business experiences that you'll find useful when making choices about starting and operating your own business.

Name: Danielle
Company: Dani J Couture
E-mail: danielle@danijcouture.com
Website: www.danijcouture.com

Since I was a little girl, I have always loved to shop. I remember going through clothing department stores with my aunt grabbing everything my little hands could hold. So as I grew older and started thinking about what I wanted to do in life, I figured what better path to take than fashion. I began taking sewing classes in high school, and went on to study fashion design in college. Everything was very hands on, and there was just so much to learn; the process was difficult, but so well worth it. I now have the pleasure of saying I have my own clothing line. I may not be at the top yet, but I'm on my way, so Gucci and Versace better watch out for Dani J Couture. I focus on the different styles all over the world, and then I add my own creative genius to produce unparalleled couture garments for women.

I've always had an entrepreneurial spirit, so it wasn't long after graduating from college that I realized I wanted to start my own business. I began participating in as many fashion shows as possible, and networking. I cannot stress how important networking is in any industry. You never know whom you may meet or what they may have to offer. One day you may come across the CEO of a major company, and they have the power to take you from just being a name on a stack of résumés, to the owner of the front office with a window view. I look forward to every new person I meet along the way, and use that as an opportunity to showcase my talent.

The journey has been filled with obstacles, but for every obstacle there is triple the pleasure. Starting a business requires a lot of planning, patience, and focus. I surround myself with people and objects that will preserve my motivation and keep my creative juices flowing.

A typical day for me starts out with me getting up to go to my 9 to 5 job; no matter what, the bills have to be paid. I go to class two nights a week, because there is always more to learn about business. Majority of my nights and weekends are spent designing. I know all of my hard work will pay off very soon, so I don't mind the temporary sacrifices I have to make. I have learned a lot along the way, and I wouldn't trade my experiences, good or bad, for anything in the world. They have taught me to be humble, stay focused, and be successful. To everyone who has a dream, just keep believing in yourself, because it starts with you. Set goals, challenge yourself, and keep pushing. Most important, don't get discouraged, because there is a light at the end of every tunnel. And for all you *fashionistas* out there, check out my work at www.DaniJCouture.com, Couture Me, Couture Yourself!?

* * * * * * * * * * * * *

Name: Blake
Company Name: Blake's Nanny Services
E-mail: Blakecrosby2@gmail.com
Website: www.tumblr.com/blakedc.com

I am a professional nanny for Washington, DC elite. When people hear the word nanny they automatically dismiss it as an easy occupation, when in actuality it requires experience, higher education, and certification. I currently have a long list of clients, but that did not occur over night. I had to be a true hustler, especially when it came to convincing wealthy people that I can care for and protect their children.

So, how did I build my clientele? I used three websites, word of mouth, and advertisements. First, I selected websites designed for families looking for caregivers and caregivers looking for employment opportunities. On the site, I applied for a background check to show families I was never in any legal trouble. I wrote a short blurb about my qualifications, my parenting style, and why I was an asset to their family. Next, I provided potential clients a list of references that included names and contact information of people who knew me personally and those I worked for who could speak about me professionally. The second thing I did was network to increase my clientele. I used "word of mouth" to spread the word. I openly shared with my clients that I wanted to grow my clientele. They were happy to pass on the word to other parents, friends, and acquaintances. Finally I invested in advertisements, I made business cards, passed them out, and designed fliers I hung in local parks, public venues, and local merchants where the caliber of people I sought after would frequent. The combination of all those efforts created a buzz around my name and it brought me very high-end clientele.

While that sounds all peaches and cream, being an entrepreneur does have its drawbacks. Here are a few tips on how to keep things easy breezy. (1) Don't be afraid to decline a job. If you don't see yourself happy in a position, do not waste your time by taking it. (2) Be firm when it comes to your prices. You may think lowering prices may get more business, however it can also cause your product to lose value. (3) Do not give a client any reason to doubt your product. That means never be late, stay flexible, and always be personable. If someone irritates you, suck it up and kill them with kindness. Word of mouth can help you and also hinder you. In conclusion, once you decide what you want to do, stick to it. Never second-guess yourself because once you do that, you diminish your potential for success.

I am also a motivational speaker and my website is www.tumblr.com/blakedc.com.

Visit me there. Good luck and stick with it.

· · · · · · · · · · · · ·

Name: Hans
Company Name: Groceries2GoNow
E-mail: hbeja5@hotmail.com

October 2010 while watching college football, I was thinking about ways to start a business. My cousin and I came up with an idea to start a grocery delivery service. After much thought and planning to include marketing strategies we opened on January 10, 2011.

Business was picking up at a rapid pace; however, our biggest issue was hiring people who were willing to help the business grow. My partner and I had full-time jobs while managing the business. This made things fairly difficult for us to do all the things required to be successful. Our business began to suffer because the employees we hired did not take their jobs seriously and did not provide the quality of customer service they had been trained to do. They just did not care about their job performance. Employees would show up late for work, not make the deliveries on time, and provided poor customer service.

What we learned and want to share with other aspiring entrepreneurs is that you must hire people who will take their roles and responsibilities seriously. They must be present, pleasant, and productive. You want employees to act as if their jobs are their own business.

Make sure you have the time to commit to your business, and do not expect employees to do what you would do. You must always be available to lead your employees and to ensure the business operates efficiently.

We have officially closed. The experience we gained was extremely valuable, and we do not have any bad feelings about the outcome. If I had to tell someone starting a business a valuable lesson it would be to hire people who care about your business as much as you. They are the key to your success!

. . . .

Name: David
Company Name: APE Entertainment

As a college student, I had more time on my hands than money. Several of my brothers in Alpha Phi Alpha Fraternity Inc., felt the same way. The college we attended is in a small town which really did not have a whole lot for us to do.

So one day, we jokingly started talking about starting a business. We began to talk more and more about the type of business it would be and what it would be like to be the owners. After brainstorming many ideas, we all agreed that an entertainment company would be the ideal business for us. All of us were outgoing, well known and well liked throughout the campus and in the community, and we knew through this medium, we could fulfill a community need. The community was boring and needed something new and exciting to spark the entertainment scene. We had the answer to the community's problem. We got serious and started to develop a plan.

First, we identified roles and responsibilities, second, we assigned members to the roles and responsibilities, and third, we put our plans into action. We did not have a lot of money to put into this business so we approached local club owners to negotiate leasing space for our functions. We created a marketing campaign and networked with other groups and organizations on campus, which we have always supported in their programs, i.e., fraternities, sororities, social clubs, and special groups. We appointed a treasurer to keep records, and we opened up a bank account that required two signatures. This business kept us busy and generated extra income for all of us for the remainder of our years while in college.

Most important, through this venture, we formed a bond much deeper than our fraternal bond that has kept us close beyond college, and continues to this very day.

. . . .

Name: Misty
Company Name: Misty Blue Fashion
E-mail: mistybluefashion@gmail.com
Website: mistybluefashion.wix.com/wwwmistyblue

The dream I had as a teen is starting to come true. I started college in 2004. I went to school for Fashion Design, which had been a long time dream of mine. It was not my first time in college but finally I figured out exactly what I wanted to do. After four hard years and lots of fantasies of being rich and famous, I graduated in 2008 with honors. I was not able to find a job in the fashion industry and had to take a job in a call center. After nine months I finally landed a job in the fashion industry. I learned a wealth of information for producing garments.

When I was four months pregnant I was laid off and had to go back and do what I did in college, waitress. I would then go home and make my designs. I still pursued my dream. I realized it wasn't going to happen the way I thought or as fast as I thought but still I wanted my dream to come true. I decided long ago that no matter how long it took, I will have my own clothing line and nothing was going to stop, discourage, or defeat me. Once my daughter was born, I wasn't in a big hurry to go back to waitressing. My husband and I decided that we would live off of his income alone even though we would be living at poverty level. Why? I wanted to raise my own child and have my own business. I was no longer in a hurry because I had realized it is not the destination but the journey. In this way temporarily we would live at poverty level, but I knew eventually my business would grow and things would be better. Also I knew that the journey would be happier this way. My daughter is now 3, almost 4, and I am always complimented on how well behaved and intelligent she is. As for my business, well, I will be going into production of my jeans very soon. I am blessed and I am enjoying the journey and because I will also enjoy the destination.

. . . .

Name: Victoria
Company Name: English Tutoring Service

The summer following my graduation from high school, I found myself extremely excited about starting my new life at Spellman College that upcoming fall. However, I found that finding a summer job with no prior work experience was nearly impossible for me. I applied to work at a couple stores in the mall, to be an office assistant at a few buildings in downtown Washington, DC and even had an interview at a large advertising firm, but nothing panned out. At this point, all I could do was sit down, look at my résumé, and try and assess what my background had prepared me for up until this point. I knew two things for sure. The first was that I had become a professional student in that I had developed all the tools necessary to be successful in school. Secondly, I knew that I had learned how to pass on those skills to other kids during high school while volunteering as a tutor at an after-school program in my neighborhood. Once I made this realization, I knew that working as a personal tutor would be the best option for me over the summer.

The first thing I did was go online and research how other teenagers were able to start their own tutoring business. After I did my initial bit of research, I found out that there were some important questions I had to answer before I began this new venture. I had to decide how I was going to market myself and find clients. I decided to utilize the Internet to do just that. I made a profile on a popular tutoring and babysitting website, opened a new bank account, and began to network with families. After a few days, I had a series of interviews set up and before I knew it, I had a steady flow of clients and families that I have now been working with over the last three summers. I was even able to take my business overseas. While studying abroad in Seoul, South Korea last fall I was able to find work as an English language tutor. This enabled me to make some spending money to use while in Korea and I even had some savings left over to pay for school expenses for my next semester. By starting my own tutoring business, I learned the importance of assessing my own unique skills by using them in a way that is both efficient and true to me.

Famous Entrepreneurs Who Started in their Teens

The famous entrepreneurs featured here were also teens when they launched their bold ideas.

After reading their stories, you will see they share a common theme with the entrepreneurs in the previous stories. Their success also started with a skill or talent that they were passionate about, and all of them refused to let setbacks, unfortunate events, and the lack of resources stop them.

Both sets of entrepreneurs share these common traits: belief, confidence, creativity, financial savvy, motivation, persistence, positivity, problem-solving, resilience, resourcefulness, and risk-taking. These qualities helped them get paid forward. They used two important aspects of human capital wisely: they reached out to help others, and they got others involved who had the skills or talents needed for them to achieve their goals.

To have a successful business or career, be sure to recognize, respect, and seek the assistance of others. Seeking the skills and talents that you may be lacking is not an acknowledgment of your deficiencies but rather recognition that the team approach produces win-win results.

For example, you may be a great organizer but lack financial skills. For that reason, you'd seek out others who have the financial skills you require to be successful. Using and valuing other's skills and talents, increases your opportunity to succeed. You can't be successful standing on an island alone. Seeking others who have the skills and talents you need to prosper will produce the results you desire.

Learn to appreciate others' gifts and show gratitude, giving that same appreciation and gratitude to yourself when times are hard. If you view problems as challenges, it will get you closer to your dreams. Never give up on yourself.

Name: Mark Elliot Zuckerberg
Company: Facebook

Mark Zuckerberg is an entrepreneur, computer programmer, and philanthropist who developed an interest in computers at an early age. He designed a messaging program called Zucknet for his father's business, and his family used it to communicate in the home.

As Mark transitioned in his studies, he continued to follow his love for programming. While a college student, he designed the social networking site known as Facebook along with four others—an idea born in his dorm room.

Today, Mr. Zuckerberg is chairman and CEO of Facebook, Inc. and is known as the youngest self-made millionaire. Reportedly, he is worth more than a billion dollars. Facebook may be the most successful website ever built.

Read more about Mr. Zuckerberg at
en.wikipedia.org/wiki/Mark_Zuckerberg.

* * * * * * * * * * * *

Name: Frederick "Fred" DeLuca
Company: Subway Franchise

Fred DeLuca decided at the age of 17 that he wanted to be an entrepreneur. He needed to earn money to help pay for college. So he borrowed $1,000 from a friend to open up a sandwich shop. His goal was to start a fast-food venture that provided healthier, less fattening choices.

Today, there are more than 32,000 Subway locations around the world. It's been reported Subway netted 2.5 billion in 2012. Read more about Mr. DeLuca at
encyclopedia.jrank.org/articles/pages/
6179/DeLuca-Fred.html

* * * * * * * * * * * *

Name: Bill Gates
Company: Microsoft

Bill Gates's interest in computers started at an early age. As a seventh grader, he studied computers, and in high school, he and a friend started a firm. Their hard work and success landed him a job offer that he actually turned down.

Mr. Gates knew he wanted to be at the forefront of computer software design, so he dropped out of college and co-founded Microsoft with a friend. Through perseverance, he was prepared when the opportunity presented itself in 1980. He was asked by IBM to work on its personal computer project, and the rest is history. Mr. Gates developed the Microsoft Disk Operating System known today as MS-DOS. This operating system controls the way computers function.

If Mr. Gates had not stayed committed to his passion, the world would not be communicating in the manner it does today. His competitive drive and fierce desire to win has made him a powerful force in business. In 1997, his worth was estimated at approximately 37 billion. He has earned the title of richest man in America.

Read more about Mr. Gates at:
www.notablebiographies.com/Fi-Gi/Gates-Bill.

* * * * * * * * * * * *

Name: Russell Simmons
Company(s): Def Jam, Phat Farm, Rush Communications, and Run Athletics

Russell Simmons, an entrepreneur and philanthropist, applied his street smarts, knowledge of promoting music, communication, and networking skills to start several lucrative businesses.

Mr. Simmons began his music career in a group called The Force. The band made its name putting on block parties in Harlem and Queens, New York. Then he took the experience learned from his music career and applied it to promoting music. He rented venues, negotiated with acts, and promoted his own concerts.

In his early days as an entrepreneur, Mr. Simmons experienced some failures but didn't give up. At one point, he lost all of his money promoting a party and an unexpected angel who believed in him handed him money to replace it—enough to get him started again. That angel was his mother.

Mr. Simmons paid it forward and started working with his brother's hip-hop group, Run-DMC. Today, he's known as the "Godfather of Hip Hop" and has brought hip-hop music— along with the urban culture it represents—to the American mainstream. He has been successful in the launch of many businesses. Read more about Mr. Simmons at

www.lemonadestories.com/defjam.html.

• • • • • • • • • • • • •

Name: Sean Combs
Company(s): Bad Boy Records, Sean John Clothing Line, Ciroc Vodka, and Restaurant Owner

Sean Combs is an American rapper, record producer, media executive, musician, actor, and entrepreneur. Mr. Comb was fascinated with rap music since the age of 12. He would sneak out of his house to listen to and hang around rappers.

As a college student, his love for rap music continued to grow and he began to promote rap music events in the Washington, D.C. area. A friend convinced him to seek an internship with a music company and it turned out to be profitable. A company executive recognized his abilities and, in a short time, promoted him to Director of Artists and Repertoire, a position of extraordinary influence for a twenty-year-old.

Mr. Combs's keen understanding of the city's flourishing rap scene helped him secure the vice president position. He quickly became an accomplished producer, working on such successful Uptown releases as Jodeci's *Forever My Lady* and Mary J. Blige's *What's the 411?*

Mr. Combs experienced a setback when he was fired from the company, but it didn't stop him. Within two weeks, he finalized a distribution deal with a large music conglomerate. In 2012, *Forbes* magazine estimated Mr. Combs' net worth at $550 million, making him the richest figure in hip hop.

Read more at

www.answers.com/topic/sean-combs#ixzz2LBJbyUP0

In Closing

I appreciate the brave, creative, and amazingly persistent people who shared their stories with me and with you for this book. Their experiences make realizing your dreams something you can visualize and believe in *because it happened for others*. I encourage you to dream big and be a doer.

If you decide to create your own job by starting a business, keep in mind the lessons shared by these young entrepreneurs.

Also, visit www.newbeeginning.com to sign up for the teen's monthly newsletter. It features articles on how to start your own business as well as stories from other entrepreneurs. Its topics touch on life skills that will help you become happy, healthy, and productive citizens.

Conclusion

The ideas in this book will help get your foot in the next door you try!

My intentions are for you, the job seeker, to understand that *no one is trying to change you*. However, to conduct a successful job search and land that desired job or get the breaks you need to succeed, be willing to make changes on your own. Why? Because society has expectations and unwritten rules you must be aware of and willing to adhere to before you can be successful.

This book has given you a thorough introduction to the job search process. It has informed you of actions you need to take to become successful. It has equipped you with the tools needed for conquering situations as they apply to your job searches.

As a result of reading these chapters and doing the exercises, your confidence has likely increased. I hope any rumors or negative stories you've heard about job searching no longer daunt you. Now, you feel ready to go out and conquer that job or create your own.

If you follow the common rules set by the work world you're entering, I know with all my heart you will succeed.

Increase your network by connecting online at www.newbeeginning.com, or send an e-mail message to info@newbeeginning.com. Send in your job search stories and concerns. Or simply e-mail me if you need a cheerleader. Know that you are not alone. My blessings go with you.

—Naomi Vernon

Congratulations!

Each member of the group is successful in his or her own way. By following the steps outlined in this guide, they learned *job search skills* that will serve them throughout their lives. They now know how to fish; no one will ever have to give them a fish, again.

A lifetime of success awaits them!

You, too, will go a long way based on taking time to implement the ideas in this book. Now that you have the job search skills, information, and knowledge, you can see success around the corner.

Go out there and get it!